BOBBY'S TRIALS CHRONICLES
BOOK TWO

RENEGADE BARRISTER

BOBBY WILSON, JD

Publisher: Apache Publishing Company
www.apachepublishingcompany.com

ISBN-13: 9780615554617
ISBN-10: 061555461X
Library of Congress Control Number: 2011919350
Apache Publishing Company Apache Junction, AZ

DEDICATION

To my lovely wife, the woman who gives me the courage to face each new day with its various trials and tribulations.

ACKNOWLEDGMENTS

Since writing any book is an arduous and time consuming business, it is only possible with the support and great editorial contributions of others. I wish to give my deepest thanks to my wife and editor, Eileen Wilson, my great neighbor and friend, Lori Cook Heyd, David Cortner and to the many others who have volunteered their valuable time and editorial advice to this project, including my daughter, Viki.

PROLOGUE

In 1973 when I started practicing law – the Country was in anti-war mode, with widespread demonstrations. Most law graduates, including myself, did not want to work for the large law firms or corporations and certainly not for "the government." We were an idealistic bunch – wanting to help the down trodden and helpless masses. The great anti-poverty movements were active and growing.

I soon discovered that good deeds and free legal services do not pay salaries or office rent and had to settle down and try to earn a living and support myself, my family and my staff.

My law practice was a general practice – and I never knew who or what was going to walk through our door next. A murder case, child custody matter, or some unsolved mystery. Some were minor cases – others were major cases that were to make new law in the State of Texas after review by some of the highest courts in the land.

In writing this book, which is as much about what happened to some of my fortunate and unfortunate clients as happened to me – I try to tell their unusual stories in layman's language and how their experiences with our legal system changed all our lives.

The judicial process, whether it is criminal or civil in nature, can and does fundamentally change a person's life. The parties involved may feel that justice prevailed or justice was denied in their case. The actions or inactions of their legal counsel often make the difference between a just or unjust outcome. Our system of justice is not self-correcting – it is a never-ending struggle between the weak and the powerful, whether they are governmental agencies and large corporations.

Bobby Wilson, JD

PREFACE

The following stories are true – some may seem too fantastic or strange to be real – but their facts are all documented in trial transcripts, court witness testimony and public records.

The real names of my clients, the other parties, and the other actors mentioned herein have been changed to protect their identities and their right to privacy. The fact situations described herein have sometimes been altered to make the stories more readable and to protect the real identities of the actors. The locations of the discussed trials and events herein and the amounts of money described in each story may or may not be accurate to protect the privacy of the characters described.

No attempt to embarrass anyone is being made and anyone embarrassed by the facts of these stories just needs to keep their embarrassment to themselves, since their real names are not used and no one will ever know any better unless they, themselves, make their identities known. No confidential client communications have been discussed or disclosed herein.

These case stories range from murder cases, to child custody, to bank fraud trials, with a safecracker and dog massacre trial thrown in for variety.

When you finish reading this book you will know how our legal system really works – or doesn't work – depending on the circumstances.

The period of time covered by this book is from the mid nineteen-seventies to the mid-eighties – which is a lifetime in a busy trial lawyer's life and the accumulation of trial notebooks.

*Roughly defined as the onset of a haughty manner coupled with
a god-like self-image, judgitis strikes unpredictably.*
Judge Lynn Ratushny

1

LAWYERS BY NATURE ARE EGOTISTICAL AND SELF-CENTERED; otherwise they would not want to be lawyers. Most judges are even worse, since they occupy positions of power over peoples' lives and fortunes and many suffer from severe cases of judgitis.

Professional jealousy is second nature to lawyers in the practice of law and they love to see another lawyer go down in flames. While doctors assist each other with business referrals, lawyers would rather sue each other, hence the shark symbol. A new lawyer learns these facts of professional life sooner or later, usually the hard way.

Almost a year had passed since all criminal charges pending against me in Oklahoma were dismissed. My law practice was growing steadily, assisted by the local newspaper coverage of the dismissal of murder charges against the young mother from Oklahoma City who had shot-gunned her former boyfriend. I was actually starting to enjoy life for a change and it seemed like my long struggle to survive was over.

One bright and sunny morning, Jean, my thirty-five year old super-efficient office manager, ushered a new client into my office.

The smartly dressed and uniformed Private First Class soldier walked into my office and announced, "I need to hire you to represent my poor mother. She's in the Tarrant County jail." He then related how his long suffering mother had finally snapped one day and shot her deadbeat husband, Roscoe, the father of her three young children, in the heart.

Jimmy looked to be about nineteen – but mature beyond his years. He was the product of an earlier relationship of his mother – her love child, by another loser.

"I hated my stepdad, the S.O.B. beat Mom and me when he was drunk, and he stayed drunk or high on weed most of the time. She became his slave so I left home and joined the Army, before *I* had to kill him."

"Did he work?" I asked.

"No, are you kidding?" he replied – his facial expressions showing his contempt for his stepdad.

"Mom worked two jobs – she cooked at one place in the mornin' and then comes home and cooked dinner for us em' and then went back to cookin' until closing time at another place. She was workin' herself to death to pay the bills and keep food on our table."

An old cliché came to my mind as he talked; "Some people are alive only because it is against the law to kill them."

"How did your stepdad get himself shot?" I asked, showing my empathy for Jimmy's opinion of Roscoe.

"Roscoe attacked her and was going to beat the hell out of her. She grabbed her .25 heater out of her purse and told him to go away, but he kept coming – so she shot him one time –an kilt him dead."

The boy waited for my response. I looked him in the eyes, "Nothing more deadly than one well-aimed bullet. Isn't that what they teach you in the army?"

"Yes sir, it sure is!" He looked at me with a question in his eyes as to how I knew so much about his infantry training. Before he could respond I spoke in a serious tone to him, "Jimmy, the going rate for defending a first degree murder case around here starts at fifty thousand dollars, and you can't afford to pay me that kind of money on a soldier's pay. Why not let your mom's court-appointed lawyer represent her? He is older and wiser than me – I have only been practicing law for a short time. Do you really want to trust your mother's life to me?"

"A bud of mine at Fort Hood told me about that murder case you had in Cleburne, Texas, where you walked that woman for shot-gunning her boyfriend at a service station. If you can do that, then you can walk my mother. Besides, no court-appointed lawyer gives a shit about my mother."

He reached in his shirt pocket and laid ten, one hundred dollar bills on my desk.

"I will pay you one thousand now and another thousand each month until I have paid you in full," he said, "But, how about twenty five thousand dollars - since we have no money".

We both knew that once his mother was found guilty or acquitted – the payments would stop. That was the real world of lawyers and their clients. I also knew that once I told the judge I was the defense lawyer for this woman, there was no backing out or withdrawal from my responsibilities, whether I ever got paid or not; and it could be a long ride with a possibly low financial return.

"Why do you think I can do a better job than her court-appointed lawyer," I asked, looking for a way out of what was surely going to be a money losing case for me.

"Because my mom has been sitting in the county jail for over two months and her appointed lawyer has never been to see her. She only received his letter saying he was appointed to represent her. He doesn't give a damn what happens to my mother."

Quite true, I thought, but did not say it. What I knew, and he suspected, was that most court-appointed lawyers were paid a maximum of two hundred dollars per day for courtroom work, with a maximum of five thousand dollars on serious felony cases. I already knew from courthouse experience that his mother was probably looking at a plea bargain agreement of ten to twenty years in prison for second-degree murder, even with her previous clean record. The D.A.'s office probably already had the paperwork ready.

"Who is taking care of your younger sisters and brother?" I asked, buying time, and trying to decide if I wanted in or out of this mess.

"Esther, my auntie, with my help," he said.

It now became very quiet in my office – it was the moment of truth. I knew I was looking at a weeklong jury trial, plus several days of pre-trial hearings on many defense motions and other matters. The case was going to be a money loser for me, but I respected this soldier's spunk in trying to save his mother's hide, even if it financially broke him. I also respected his mother's determination to earn an honest living instead of asking for some kind of public assistance for her and her children; she seemed to be a member of a dying breed.

"You going to be a career army man?" I asked.

"Yes sir – it is my home now. I ship out to Vietnam in two weeks."

I winced, it was late 1973 and our Government's war machine still needed fresh cannon fodder for its no-win meat grinder that started in 1963. What was it that President Eisenhower had warned America? "Don't ever get involved in an Asian land war." Kennedy and Johnson had not listened to those mighty words of wisdom.

Now I felt guilty – Jimmy was going to be in combat shortly and wanted the satisfaction of knowing that his mother would have a fighting chance in our criminal justice system, for which he was willing to give his life.

"Okay Jimmy – I will do my best. My fee will be twenty five thousand dollars - but no promises."

With that he snapped to attention and extended his hand to seal the deal.

My legal brain started working – "Anybody living in your mom's house now?"

"No, it was closed as a crime scene and nobody has been in there since. They have not even allowed anyone to clean it up. House is locked."

"That's good – have you got a key?"

He reached in his pocket and took out an old copper key and handed it to me, and took his leave, with a smile on his face.

By the time he left my office it was lunchtime and my staff had gone to a fast food place next door. I needed to do something with those hundred dollar bills and make sure his mother's client account was established and credited with that initial payment.

The division of labor in my office was typical of a sole practitioner. I employed three workers; one office manager who was also a skilled legal secretary - that was Jean, a married woman, who was a devout Pentecostal and my right arm. Harriet was a middle-aged and quiet, hardworking typist. Jill, our receptionist and file clerk was a man-hungry, married mother of four young boys who at the age of twenty-four just could not be happy with only one man in her life.

I found our office bank bag on Jean's desk and inserted the ten one hundred dollar bills with a note attached for Jean to credit our new client's account. A bank deposit slip in the bag caught my eye. The slip showed an itemized list of our client's checks deposited into our office operating account at our bank that morning, but there was no mention of any cash being deposited. *That's odd,* I thought, we almost always had cash payments coming into our office every day to deposit. Many of our clients did not have bank accounts and always paid in cash on their accounts.

A chill ran down my back. Someone in our office might be helping themselves to my cash receipts. It could be anyone - our cleaning man, or a brazen client who knew where we kept our bank bag, which was no secret around our office. I needed to address the issue of the missing cash; it could be a serious problem. I was too trusting, with no effective system in place to monitor cash receipts. I would need to alert our bank to watch our various accounts for any unusual activity. I needed to be careful how I handled this situation; nothing is more explosive or disruptive to a small office than announcing there is dishonesty or internal theft afoot. I needed to come up with a plan that would not cause an upheaval at my office. A night of restless sleep awaited me.

The next day I drove the twenty miles to the Tarrant County jail in *Cow Town*, Fort Worth, Texas, to meet with my new client, Sally. Fort Worth is known as the gateway to the West and it has retained its western flavor and heritage since 1849 when it was an Army outpost. It is the fifth largest city in Texas and claims no relationship to its Dallas cousin thirty miles to the east. The people and personalities of the two cities are as different as night and day, as President Kennedy discovered, too late. Cow Town has kept its old stockyards and dance halls, such as *Billy Bobs* for its tourist trade, while Dallas has preserved its *Dealey Plaza* for its tourists; need I say more?

Sally was brought down to me in the lawyer's conference room. The slamming jailhouse doors still gave me the creeps, as did that rancid smell that most county jails seem to share. My own memories of county jail life flashed through my mind.

She looked depressed, a small woman of about forty, probably weighing 110 pounds and standing five feet tall, rather frail looking. For some reason, I expected a larger, more self-confident woman, one able to raise four children while supporting her family by holding down two full-time jobs as a cook.

My first impression of this woman was of someone who could not hurt a flea, much less kill someone. I hoped a jury would feel the same.

She talked so quietly I had to tell her to speak louder. She was shy and had a speech impediment, which made it difficult to understand her. She also had a bad case of low self-esteem. I now understood why she worked as a cook and not a waitress: the public arena demands clear communication skills, something she was not blessed with.

"Your son, Jimmy hired me to defend you; he wants to do everything he can to help you in this case," I said, trying to put her at ease.

The lines in her face told me life had not been easy for her, but she smiled broadly at the mention of her son.

"Tha-tha-thank you for taking my ca-ca-case - but I have no mo-money," she managed to stutter, casting her eyes to the floor.

"You have a brave and fine son, you must be proud of him for trying to find you a lawyer," I said. Before you are fed into the justice system as fresh meat by your court-appointed lawyer, as I had almost been many years ago, I thought to myself.

She smiled broadly. I saw in her brown eyes the close bond she had with her eldest son. They were co-dependents, who had lived through some hard times together.

"How old are your other children?" I asked, trying to put her at ease.

"Ei-ei-eight, te-ten, and thir-thirteen; one boy, tw-two girls - my sister has them now. Jim-Jim-Jimmy helps her and the ki-kids as much as he ca-can."

"Tell me about your deceased husband – how long married," I asked.

"About twe-twe-twelve years – he was not an easy man to li-li-live with. He was a coo-cook when we met, but he stopped wor-wor-working years ago and went on dis-dis'bility with his ba-back. Stayed at ho-ho-home to take care of the kids while I wo-worked. He had gotten fa-fat and me-me-mean the last few years and dra-drank too much. The kids and I – we afraid of he-he-him. He would get me-mean with us. Last ye-ye-year he started seeing other wo-women while I wor-worked, leaving the kids al-al-alone. That caused a lot of fightin' between us."

"How big a man was your husband?"

"He was a bi-bi-big man, over six foot, about three hun-hun-hundred pounds."

"Were you afraid of him?"

"Yea, I tried to sta-stay way from him when he was dri-drinking or ma-mad."

"Did he ever physically attack you?"

"Yea, he would sho-shove me against the wall or sl-slap me down and threaten to ki-ki-kill me if I argued with him – he told me if I ever called the pi-pi-pigs on him, he would bur-bury me in the back yar-yard and tell the children I ran away with another ma-man."

"What happened on the day he got shot? You can tell me everything, I am your lawyer, and what you tell me can never be used against you."

"I come home from my ear-early job to fi-fix din-dinner for him and the ki-kids about three o'clock. When I came into the kit-kitchen from the outside door I could he-hear him talking to someone in the ba-back, on our bedroom ph-phone. I picked up the ph-phone in the kitchen and listened to him and he's talking to a dam' bitch– he was making a date with her for later that night – he wanted her to buy some we-weed for them to smoke when he came ov-over. When I heard that – I sh-sh-shouted in the phone for her to stay away from my ma-ma-man and Roscoe screamed at me to ha-hang up my ph-phone – and then I heard him say he would call her back later – *after he took care of his bit-bitch and her sm-smart-ass mouth*. I heard him coming toward the kit-kitchen – he was screaming, "I'm going to kick your sor-sor-sorry ass, you bitch. I clo-closed the kitchen door and put my back against the door and bra-braced myself to hold the door clo-closed. Roscoe was big-big-bigger and stronger than me and he bod-body slammed into the do-door pushing it and it was com-coming open and I couldn't keep him ou-ou-out so I gra-grabbed my purse and gra-grabbed my gu-gun and stu-stuck it through the opening in the da-doorway - told him I would shoo-shoo-shoot him if he didn't leave me alone.

He suddenly stopped pu-pushing on the door and jumped ba-back, the door slammed sh-sh-shut – catchin' my gun; he pulled the da-door cl-closed trying to ke-keep the gu-gun stuck in the door. I tried to pu-pull the gu-gun out of the door, it fir-fired and Roscoe hollered from the other side of the da-door and I heard him hi-hi-hit the flo-floor with a cra-crash. I didn't want to shoo-shoot him, the gu-gun was stuck in the door-doorway and I was trying to pu-pull it out when it fi-fired. The da-door was shut when the gu-gu-gun fired, I couldn't see he-him on the other si-side, but the bull-bullet hit him and he fell da-da-dead on the floor - there was blood everywhere. I ca-called an ambulance – but he passed. The police arrested me for mur-murder and I have been here in jail – it has been over two months. I can't ra-raise the ba-bail, so here I sit and my ba-babies have no ma-mother or fa-father. I never meant to shoo-shoot him – I just wanted him to leave me alone."

"Why did you carry a pistol in your purse?" I asked.

"My ni-night job was in a ba-ba-bad part of town and it is a very da-dark and dangerous to be around there late at night; I was always sca-scared walking to my ca-car."

"Did you tell the police how the gun was caught in the door and you were trying to pull the gun out when it discharged?"

"Yeah, but they didn't believe me and said I just sh-sh-shot him because I heard him talking to another wo-woman; said I was just a cra-crazy jealous wife."

"Did you tell the police he was talking to his girlfriend when you came home?"

"Yea, they said I should have just di-divorced him and not sh-shot him. They arrested me in fr-front of my crying babies – the kids were screaming and trying to ho-hold onto me and were tracking blo-blood everywhere as the police pulled me away."

"What do you think would have happened to you if Roscoe had gotten his hands on you that day?"

"He would have taken the ga-ga-gun away from me and shot me or be-beat the hell out of me with it."

"Were you afraid he might kill you?"

"Yea – he was crazy ma-ma-mad. He had been drinking all da-da-day."

"How long have you been holding down two jobs?"

"About two years – Roscoe would take my mo-money and spend it on boo-booze and we-weed, I had to hi-hide some of my money in order to buy fo-fo-food and clothes for the kids."

"Who would know that?" I interrupted.

"The nei-neighbors and my sister, Esther."

Her eyes were starting to tear-up and her voice was breaking so I told her to keep her chin-up and if it was okay with her – I would file a motion for speedy trial and force the state to put her to trial and get her out of the jail as soon as possible, otherwise she could be sitting in jail for a year or more. She wholeheartedly agreed. I cautioned her that if I filed such a motion, the prosecutor would take a hostile position on her case and do her no favors or deals.

She knew she would not see daylight until her case was resolved. In the meantime her three minor children were without a parent. That created a burden to her already overloaded sister's family. She gave me her employers' names so I could talk to them about being witnesses to her defense. Also, she suggested several of her neighbors that knew her family situation.

I watched her closely and tried to look at her as a potential juror would. She appeared to be a shy woman by nature – often casting her eyes to the floor as she spoke to me. A juror could take that appearance several ways – she was shy and afraid, or she was being untruthful and evasive in her answers. Her stutter and low voice bothered me and I suspected would irritate many jurors. I would need her to testify to what occurred that day and most jurors would not have much patience with a witness they could not understand or who would not look them in the eye. She would not be a strong witness.

I looked at her hands and they told me a story – worn and rough – a workingwoman. I would want the jury to look at those small worn hands. Juries respect a person who works for a living and tries their best to support their family. Texas juries also have little respect for lazy, two-timing pot smoking spouses. At least this time I did not have to worry about a prosecutor throwing a prior criminal record in my client's face if she took the witness stand. She was clean – thank God for that.

I always believed that a murder defendant must take the stand in his or her own defense – no matter how bad a criminal record they have. A jury must realize the defendant is a human being and not just a name; otherwise there is *no connection* between that jury and that defendant, which means – no empathy, and a probable conviction.

A defense attorney must put the jury in the defendant's shoes at the time of the violent encounter – and make the jury wrestle with that old cliché: *But for the grace of God, there go I.*

"Sally, do you know the name of the woman Roscoe was talking to that day on the phone?"

"No, I didn't recognize her va-va-voice – she sounded ya-younger than me."

I made a mental note to subpoena my client's phone records and track down the other woman – and then subpoena her to trial. Focus the jury's attention on the lifestyle of the dead husband and *other woman*, instead of on my client. I would need to try to make my client's case without her having to testify, if at all possible. She would be a weak witness in her own defense.

The other woman would probably take the "Fifth" on advice of the prosecutor and refuse to testify because of the illegal drug angle – which would be ok with me – jurors hate witnesses who take the stand and then refuse to testify.

I would then ask the other woman who advised her to take the "Fifth" and caused her to refuse to testify and the prosecutor would surely immediately object and the judge sustain – but the jury would smell a rat and the state would take a hit.

Sally related to me how bad it was in that jail. I told her to not get into trouble and just be patient; it would all be over in a few weeks.

I hated jails, any jail, city, county, and prisons. They all gave me butterflies in the stomach and they all had *that smell*. I would never be comfortable being in a jail to visit a client – it dredged up bitter memories in my past. I would always smile to myself when clients would relate how *bad* things were in their place of confinement – the food, the odors, the guards, and the fellow prisoners who abused them. I would shake my head knowingly – but never shared my own jailhouse experience with any client.

I bid Sally goodbye and she smiled for the first time – with hope in her brown eyes. I needed to find a way to get her story before the jury without calling her as a witness; she would become mush when under attack on the stand by an aggressive prosecutor, besides the problem with her stutter.

Over the next week I notified the criminal court judge and the prosecutor's office of my involvement and I filed the usual many motions for discovery in order to see and review all of the prosecutor's evidence against my client. Past appellate court decisions in Texas required the state prosecutor to allow the defense attorney to see and review all evidence the state planned to use against the defendant, plus any evidence that might indicate the innocence of the defendant – even if the prosecutor was not going to use that evidence in court, to do otherwise was reversible error on behalf of the state's attorney.

I reviewed all the police and crime scene reports and they basically related that a "Jealous wife shot her husband after a domestic fight in their home." Nothing was stated about possible self-defense or an accidental discharge of the pistol in question during the confrontation.

I filed a motion to examine the house in question and the prosecutor responded saying they had no further need to secure the premises and it was released to the family to "use and enjoy".

I drove to Sally's three bedroom frame house before anyone could destroy the possible evidence still inside. A defense attorney should always personally view an alleged crime scene; he needs to know its most intimate details in order to know if the testifying police investigators or the prosecutor are being truthful with their evidence.

I unlocked the front door and was immediately greeted by a rancid stench – a mixture of rotting food, dirty clothing, and blood. Sally's house was as if the shooting had occurred only a day earlier. The entire kitchen entryway floor and door were covered with a thick layer of dark dried blood – a full body load. My head began to spin and I found a kitchen chair to sit in until I gained my composure. The scene and smell was too close for comfort to me from my own past experiences.

Roscoe's lifeblood must have squirted like a water hose from his chest wound as he rapidly expired in a giant pool of his own blood. Whoever said a .25 caliber automatic was a useless *popgun* needed to see what I saw. It was common knowledge among gun fanciers that these types of small caliber bullets often bounced off bones or failed to enter the hard areas of the human body – such as skulls and chest cavities – but this one bullet certainly tore a big hole in Roscoe's heart.

I closely examined the door and the doorframe from both sides. Sure enough, there was the outline of a gun barrel visible on the kitchen side of the door and a matching gun barrel indentation on the doorframe attached to the wall.

Even more telling – a small bullet groove showed where the gun barrel was located when it discharged its deadly bullet. It was truly remarkable that this one low velocity bullet still had sufficient force to enter Roscoe's chest cavity. This guy's luck certainly ran out on that day. If the bullet had hit his large body anywhere else but where it did, he would probably only been slightly injured and he would be the one claiming self-defense after he did serious harm to his wife.

There is no better evidence in a civil or criminal trial than physical evidence. A jury will always rely on physical evidence over any witness testimony. I found the so-called smoking gun proof that the barrel of my client's gun was caught between the door and doorframe at the time it fired its fatal bullet. There were now grounds for reasonable doubt to be established in this case.

I retrieved some tools from my car and after taking photos from different viewpoints of the door and doorway, I removed the inside doorframe and the door itself and carefully wrapped them with some old sheets I found in the house. I wrote the date and time and my name on the sheet and tied everything together with rope and put it in a locked storage unit at my office.

Several days later I visited with the Assistant District Attorney handling the state's case against Sally. He was a former college football tackle and was a physically large man built like a bulldog with a matching personality.

Before I could explain to him my client's good work and family history and the facts of the case – he handed me a plea bargain agreement and said, "Best offer, 10-15 years in prison – 2nd degree murder, credit for time served."

"It's a case of self-defense which was really an accidental shooting," I protested.

"Bullshit, take it or leave it," he said and glared, waiting for my response.

"See you in court." I stood up, handing him a copy of my motion for speedy trial which I filed as I took my leave from the courthouse. Under Texas law, once a motion for speedy trial was filed on behalf of an incarcerated defendant – the state is under time limits and must put that person on trial within a short period or the court must dismiss the case. Of course, many prosecutors and judges take such motions as a personal affront and professional courtesies are set aside by all - and the case is set for immediate trial in a hostile atmosphere.

Several weeks later a jury was selected, sworn and seated. Selection of a jury in a criminal case is more of a game of chance than most people realize, it is a process of elimination rather than selection.

A jury panel of about fifty good citizens of the county is called into the courtroom for jury selection, which hopefully will result in the seating of twelve good and fair-minded jurors.

The prosecutor and defense lawyer are allowed to question those potential jurors, but only with previously prepared questions that the judge has already approved.

I needed a jury composed of people who knew what it was to work for a living and try to raise a family at the same time. I also needed a God-fearing jury that did not condone drinking, pot smoking, and cheating spouses.

The prosecutors were looking for jurors that are business people or pillars of the community, so they can deputize them to carry out the government's work and convict the accused.

The judge just wanted to move his docket, and for the trial to be over as quickly as possible, and pushed us like a cattle drover toward that goal.

Several jurors were allowed to disqualify themselves by stating they had preconceived opinions of the defendant's guilt or they or their family members had been victims of the violence.

Several of the jury panel had law enforcement backgrounds and they probably were prosecution leaning – but they of course, denied any prejudice against the defendant. I used all my challenges to strike the obvious pro-prosecution jurors.

The prosecutor and defense lawyer are each allowed to strike a certain number of jurors for no reason at all and after all those strikes and other disqualifications are done – the *first* twelve jurors remaining become the jury – so there is no real jury "selection" that takes place, there is really a jury by elimination seated.

The end result was a jury that was hard to read, capable of anything.

After the jury was seated in Sally's case, the prosecutor gave his opening statement to the jury that "Sally had murdered her defenseless husband in cold blood in his own home in a jealous rage when she caught him talking to another woman on the phone."

I waived an opening address – asking the court for permission to wait until the state rested its case-in-chief. That was my right and did not want to forewarn the prosecution concerning my trial plans. I was planning to introduce that door and doorframe into evidence when it became a point of contention after I cross-examined the state's witnesses as to their failure to note such important evidence of an accidental shooting in their reports.

The prosecutor's medical and technical witnesses quickly proved Roscoe was shot with Sally's pistol. The medical examiner proved Roscoe was shot in the heart and died instantly from a single .25 caliber bullet.

Then the police investigation team testified to their findings and my client's *excited utterances* that she shot him because he was talking to his girlfriend on the phone.

The state offered into evidence the weapon of death and its one battered bullet, without any objection from me.

On cross-examination of the crime scene investigators I set the stage for introduction of the door and doorframe itself into evidence.

"Did your team find any bullet holes in the kitchen door?" I asked.

"No – that's why we knew she was lying to us about them struggling with the door, there were no bullet holes in the door – so she was facing him when she shot him, *deliberately*" – the witness took his free shot at my client without my objection.

"Is it possible that Roscoe shut the kitchen door on the gun barrel and it was caught and wedged between the door and doorframe and the gun was actually stuck there when it fired?" I asked and waited for the prosecutor's objection to my speculative question, which did not come.

"Impossible," was the investigating officer's immediate response, my trap sprung open. I showed the officer the photos I had made of both sides of the subject door and he admitted that he recognized the subject door with its blood bath on one side. Then I brought into the courtroom the actual door and the doorframe and had it marked as trial exhibits, all over the heated objections from the prosecutor, which the judge overruled. The judge and jury now sat on the edges of their seats to get a better look at my large items of evidence, which obviously the red-faced prosecutor did not want them to see and examine.

"Officer – do you recognize the door and doorframe involved in this case – complete with blood splatter on the entry side?"

"Yes, that's it," was his weak reply. He knew trouble was coming his way.

"Officer, examine that door and doorframe closely and see if you have an opinion if there is an imprint of the barrel of this .25 automatic pistol between the door and doorframe?"

The officer picked up the pistol and placed it in the groove created when the door and doorframe was closed together, it clearly fit. The jury was transfixed with this evidence.

"Hard to say what caused that groove, maybe the gun, maybe not," the investigator said, his face turning red.

It was obvious to everyone in the courtroom that the pistol's barrel was imprinted on the door and doorframe and was a perfect match. The judge stared at me with a worried look in his eyes. The jurors exchanged looks.

I offered into evidence the doorframe and kitchen door. The prosecutor objected loudly, but the judge agreed with me that the jury needed to examine those items and make their own determination.

The state then rested their case, and the judge overruled my motion to direct a verdict of acquittal.

I then gave my opening statement; basically outlining the shooting was accidental in nature. A small, frail woman in fear of her life had pulled her small pistol only to protect herself from death or serious bodily injury from an attacking brute of a man. The gun was caught between the kitchen door and doorframe when her husband slammed the door shut and tried to trap the weapon in the doorframe. It had discharged accidently. Even more telling, her husband had been caught making a date for later that night with his pot smoking lover and was heard to tell his girlfriend he was about to *attack* his wife.

My first witnesses were her two employers who testified without objection that she was an honest, dependable, hardworking woman. They also both testified that Sally still had her job if she wanted it. I saw the jury exchange glances at that testimony; the case was no longer a one-way trip to the big house for Sally. The jury now realized they were sitting in judgment on a decent human caught up in a violent encounter with a worthless husband.

I called Leroy Brown, Sally's next-door neighbor, who testified he had known Sally for many years and had watched her raise and care for her family and work many hours to support them. More important, he heard and saw Roscoe's drunken ranting and his mistreating of Sally and the children. Leroy also related his prior complaints to Roscoe to stop peeing in his backyard within clear view of his family. The jury stirred uncomfortably with that testimony.

I next called Clara Scott, another neighbor, whose house was across the street and faced Sally's house. Clara related how she would watch Roscoe leave his house at night and get into a car driven by an unknown woman and that vehicle would not return until shortly before Sally returned from her night job. "Roscoe was obviously under the influence, and would stumble into his house," she related. Clara said, "I knew Sally was at work on those nights and Sally's young children were home alone after Roscoe drove away with his lady friend."

Of course, the state's attorney objected long and hard to my witnesses testifying about matters he considered irrelevant and immaterial to the killing, but the judge agreed with me that Sally's *state of mind* at the time was relevant to the issue of intent to kill and the family's social relationship was relevant.

I then called the subpoenaed girlfriend of the dead man. She looked the part, a younger, cheaply dressed woman who was very nervous and would not look at the jury or me. She only looked at the prosecutor, who looked away.

"What is your name, ma'am", I asked.

"I refuse to answer – claimin' my rights," she said in a sheepish voice. "My rights to not say nuthin'," she replied, still looking at the prosecutor for assistance.

I looked at the judge; he looked at his watch.

The judge announced: "It is time to quit for the day," and quickly adjourned court until the following morning, telling the jury not to discuss the case among themselves or anyone else.

"All counsel and the defendant to remain in the courtroom." He excused the witness to go. "Better be back here at nine o'clock in the morning," he shot her a glare and she quickly took her leave, sweat starting to bead on her forehead.

When the courtroom was empty except for the judge, prosecutors, Sally, and me, the judge – an older west Texas character who had been on the criminal bench for over twenty years and endured hundreds of felony trials – but could have passed himself off easily as a sunburned rancher – looked at the prosecutor with a frown on his face.

"Greg – you overcharged on this case – this is no murder case – maybe manslaughter, if even that. This jury is going to hang-up sure as hell and all our time and work is going to be wasted. There is now reasonable doubt in my mind about this shooting."

The prosecutor's face slowly turned bright red.

The judge leaned forward across the bench, "I would approve a plea bargain for involuntary manslaughter, one year in jail which will be probated for two years, credit for time served. What do you say defense counsel?"

The judge was looking hard at me now – frowning – but with a twinkle in his eyes.

My mind was racing, my client's future was in my hands, and I had to be very careful. "I want my client released from jail. She has three minor children to care for and she is their sole support. Both her employers say they will put her back to work".

My biggest fear about putting my client on the stand was a question that I knew the state's attorney was sure to ask and my client would probably look like a deer caught in on-coming headlights – "Why did you not just run out the door and call the police when you heard your husband threaten you on the phone?" There was no battered spouse defense in Texas at that time and under Texas law my client was under a legal obligation to retreat before using deadly force; I knew such a jury instruction would probably be allowed by the judge to go into the jury's deliberations. I was sure my client did not intend to kill her husband, but it did not matter what I thought, only what the jury thought. The judge was probably correct, this case was heading for a mistrial and my client was going back to jail, for months probably.

"If the prosecutor would offer her a one year sentence, probated for one year with credit for her jail time already served, and no fine or probation fees, and she can go home tonight, we could live with that," I announced to the court after conferring with Sally and explaining what she faced if she testified and the case ended in a mistrial.

I looked at the beaten prosecutor – he quietly said, "Okay, let's do it."

My client was smiling and standing tall before the bench when the judge advised her she was pleading guilty to involuntary manslaughter and would be on probation for one year, with no court supervision or fees to pay. The judge further said, "In six months if you stay out of trouble I will dismiss this case and you will have no conviction on your record – can you behave that long?"

"Ya-ya-yes, sir," Sally said as tears rolled down her face.

After the old judge made everything official, he adjourned court and walked down from his bench and gave Sally a big hug and told her to "Go take care of your babies."

I had never seen or heard of a judge doing that before, or since.

"Tha-tha-thank you, sir, and go-go-God bless," Sally managed to say.

I stayed at the county jail long enough to see that she was processed out of jail quickly and her sister was there to pick her up, she gave me a tearful hug and said she and Jimmy would mail me a check every month until she was paid-up. I smiled, and told her to get back on her feet first, and then worry about her bill.

I drove back to my office exhausted and tried to refocus my mind on addressing my office theft issue, a very unpleasant matter that could not be ignored any longer.

If there were no bad people there would be no good lawyers.
Charles Dickens

2

LAW SCHOOLS DO NOT TEACH A LAWYER how to manage and operate a law office. He or she either goes to work for a firm that already has in place a management team and office procedures, or, the new practitioner learns law office management and procedures through experience – which can have an expensive and stressful learning curve. I had turned down opportunities to work for established law firms – which was probably a mistake since I needed some role models in office management.

I started keeping my eyes on our office bank bag. I was watching for missing cash. It did not take long to discover that more cash was coming into my office than was being deposited into our various bank accounts. Unlike many business owners, I never removed cash from my cash receipts and *all* revenue coming into my office was to be deposited at our bank. To do otherwise was an invitation for the office staff to also help themselves and tax problems with the IRS caused by an unhappy employee or client looking for revenge. I made it my office policy not to cheat on my taxes or flirt with the office personnel. I had learned while working in the grocery business to keep my *meat and potatoes separate,* unless you wanted an old flame to turn on you one day and cause you great pain and embarrassment. Such behavior had ruined many a lawyer or other professional. I also wanted no problems with the tax people.

It was still a mystery to me about who was the guilty party or parties. It was possible that two or more of my staff were in cahoots. Jean, my office manager was married to a Pentecostal preacher and had two teenage children. Her husband sold life insurance part-time to bring in extra income. She had money problems, but had freely told me and had actually borrowed several hundred dollars from me weeks earlier to supposedly help them with their mortgage payments. She dressed conservatively in the Pentecostal manner and seemed to be a deeply religious person. She was an excellent legal assistant with a vast knowledge of real estate and domestic relations law; I wanted very much to dismiss her as a suspect, because she was vital to my office.

Harriet was a quiet hardworking secretary who was married to a retired engineer. She did not appear to have any money problems; and was too timid for me to suspect her of being a thief. She did not seem to have the nerve for it.

That left Jill, the receptionist, who was the person who accepted our clients' payments, wrote receipts, credited their accounts, and then turned the checks and cash over to Jean to make the daily bank deposits. She was the first to handle the cash and she could easily just credit the clients' accounts and stick some of any cash payments into her pocket and Jean would not even be aware of the missing money. She was the prime suspect, especially since I had learned that she was spending money for gifts on her various boyfriends without her husband's knowledge.

I needed to be sure before I accused anyone, so I called a client I trusted and asked him to do me a favor. Bring one hundred twenty dollars in cash to my office tomorrow and pay it on his account. I told him to write in small red letters his date of birth on each bill and make sure he got a receipt for his cash payment at my office.

All three of my employees had their personal bank accounts at the same bank as our office's business accounts. I called our bank and talked to the president and told him in confidence the problem I had and he agreed to have his staff keep separate envelopes of all deposits made by my office and any deposits made by my three employees. My trap was set, now I waited to see who got caught. It did not take long.

The following afternoon, after the office closed, I looked in the bank bag at that day's deposit slips and discovered only twenty dollars in cash had been deposited into the office accounts, everything else deposited were checks. I called the bank president who was waiting for my call. His deposit envelopes told the tale. The twenty dollars cash deposited that day revealed the red lettered date of birth. Only one of my employees had made a deposit into their bank accounts that day, and that was Jean. She had deposited one hundred dollars in cash, the bills each having the telltale red date of birth written on them. A sick feeling ran through my stomach, which turned to anger when I remembered I had fully trusted her and had freely loaned her money in the past, which she had never repaid. I felt like a man who had caught his wife with another man; utter betrayal.

I had no idea how much money had been stolen, but I suspected it could be quite large, since Jean had worked for me almost a year and much cash had passed through our office during that time. Now, I knew why it seemed that the harder I worked the less money I made at the end of each month - Jean was my silent partner.

I called my CPA and requested him to perform a secret audit of my office's cash receipts as compared with actual cash deposited in our bank accounts over the past six months. The audit was to be done afterhours and on the weekends to avoid my staff knowing about it. It would take a week to complete. Needless to say, it was a long and uncomfortable week. My staff knew something was afoot, but no one said anything.

And, since in real life, *when it rains it pours,* I received a phone call from the wife of my office janitor. She told me that he had suffered a heart attack and was now totally and permanently disabled. He had cleaned our office every weekday night; I now had to deal with that vacancy.

When I informed the ladies of the office about our lack of a janitor, Jean immediately volunteered to take over the cleaning responsibility for the same pay as the janitor since *she needed extra income*. That put me on the spot, which is what she wanted to do. If I told her "no", she would know I was on to her; if I said "yes", she would have an excuse to come and go from the office at night when the auditor was working.

"Okay," I said, "but, our CPA will be working at night on our books trying to determine if we need to incorporate our business for tax purposes, so you will have to clean around him while he works." I don't think I fooled anyone, even though my statement was partially true.

The office became quite somber and quiet for the remainder of the week and I noticed that Jean's cleaning efforts were half-hearted at best. The CPA finished his audit that Friday night and announced to me after hours his startling findings – forty thousand dollars in missing cash! I talked the matter over with the CPA and he was confident that, if necessary, his audit would withstand any legal challenges.

Jean had not cleaned that particular Friday night due to her church duties, or so she said. It was just as well that she was not there when I heard the bad news; I would have fired her on the spot. She had requested and received my permission to be allowed to clean the office the next day, which was Saturday.

I spent that night drafting an agreement between Jean and I, in which she confessed to her theft. She would repay the stolen funds over a certain time period or I would turn the matter over to the local D. A. for prosecution. I planned to confront Jean when she came into the office to clean Saturday night. That night and following morning passed very slowly.

Finally, at seven o'clock Saturday night I heard Jean's voice talking to her fifteen-year-old daughter as they walked in the front door of my office. I waited in my office as I heard the vacuum cleaner start growling as it headed for my office. I wondered why she had her daughter with her, which was unusual when she cleaned. My office door slowly opened and the cute teenager stuck her head through the partially open door and asked sweetly if she could clean my office.

"Where is Jean?" I asked.

"Oh, she did not feel well and dropped me off to clean the office and said to call my dad when I was done and ready to go home."

"Oh, I see," was all the answer I could muster. "Come on in and don't mind me, I am used to working around noise." An uneasy feeling came over me.

Sidney pushed open the door and backed into my office all the while pushing the vacuum cleaner back and forth. I was shocked to see she was wearing nothing but short shorts and a skimpy halter-top. I knew Pentecostals did not wear that type of attire, ever.

This woman/child was fully developed and proud of her assets. I tried to avoid starring at her as she moved closer and closer to where I sat. She was soon leaning over my desk showing me her considerable cleavage while working her spray bottle and cleaning cloth. She looked into my eyes like a temptress and moved around the desk until she was within easy reach. The alarms started ringing in my head... this is a set-up; get the hell out.

I quickly arose, "I think I am going to call it a night, Sidney, have your parents lock up after you are finished cleaning." She looked surprised and unsure of what to say.

I did not wait for her reply and kept moving until I was at the nearest public watering hole. "Wow, that was a close one," I said out loud as I tasted the cool Weller and Water make its way down my scratchy throat.

I now realized for the first time that I was not dealing with the God-fearing people I thought they were, but with pure evilness; people who were willing to use their daughter as bait, and she being a willing participant. I needed to be very careful about the snowballing situation at my office. I began to suspect that I was only now seeing the tip of the iceberg of what had been occurring at my office. I needed to have a candid talk with Harriet and Jill before Monday, at which time Jean and I were going to have a *come to Jesus meeting*. She would be out of a job and either making restitution to me or face a grand jury indictment.

On Sunday I called Harriet and asked permission to come to her house and speak to her, with her husband present. She seemed to be expecting my call.

When I arrived I could tell by their somber faces that they already knew why I was there. I quickly told them what facts I had uncovered about what was occurring at the office.

"Harriet, I know now, I should have been more involved with managing the office, but I basically trusted Jean with everything I had. I let her run the office as she saw fit and now I realize my mistake. In complete confidence, and just between the three of us, tell me what has been going on at the office when I am not there?" I asked.

Harriet waited a few minutes to choose her words carefully. "Jean is a sick control freak, she told Jill and me that she is our boss and if we don't do exactly as she says without any question, she will physically throw us out the front door. We are very afraid of her. She tries to impress everyone with her religious beliefs, but she is nothing but a great big hypocrite. She even has a boyfriend that she supports and that is why she is always broke and needing money."

"Wow," was all I could manage as a reply. "Did you and Jill know she was taking money from the office?"

"Not for sure, but I suspected as much, because she never prepared the bank deposits when either of us were in her office, and she would not allow anyone else to touch the bank bags or make bank deposits, only her. She is not the person you think she is, she is very respectful to you to your face, but she mocks you when you are gone because you do not pay her any attention when she has her hair done-up or wears a new dress. She has a crush on you and you don't pay any attention to her."

"How does she get along with Jill?" I asked.

"She hates Jill because she is younger and more attractive, and Jean is very jealous of other men's attention to Jill even though she keeps a boyfriend on the side."

"What do you know about Jean's boyfriend?" I asked, "I have never seen her with another man."

"He only comes in the office when Jean calls and tells him you are gone for the day, he sometimes brings her lunch and they drive off together in his pickup and are gone sometimes for hours. He is a big man, about six-four, always wears black motorcycle boots and a black cowboy hat; rough looking guy. He never speaks to Jill and me and just walks straight back to Jean's office like he owns the place."

I told Harriet to come to work an hour late on Monday since I was going to be at the office at eight o'clock when Jean would arrive and find all her personal property in a cardboard box sitting on her desk. That suited Harriet fine, and I could see her relax for the first time as I thanked her for her honesty and told her not to tell anyone, even Jill, about our conversation and took my leave.

I thought back about my relationship with Jean and tried to analyze why I had come to trust her so completely and had been so blind to her true nature. I had been desperate to hire an experienced legal secretary to manage my office. I was still learning on the fly and needed someone who could put together a real estate closing and domestic relations case with all its attendant documents. Any legal assistant with those talents already had a good job and was not looking for a job. Almost on cue, Jean walked into my office one morning; unannounced, and said she was new in town. Her husband had taken the Pastor position with a local church and she needed a job and had almost ten years of experience with an east Texas law firm, doing mostly real estate and domestic relations work.

I could barely hide my excitement, what a Godsend, I must be living right, I thought to myself. Jean was dressed in a long dress, fully covering her plump body. Her long hair tightly arranged in a tight bun on top of her head. She had a friendly face and sweet outward disposition. I did not even think to ask for references, and only asked her some questions about real estate and domestic relations to which she had immediate and correct answers. I offered her a modest salary and watched for her reaction. She surprised me with an immediate acceptance and said she could start work the next morning, which was fine with me. She asked for her leave to enroll her teenage children in the local school system.

Thereafter, I was so impressed with her abilities that I essentially turned my office over to her, including paying the office bills and handling all of our banking business. I was glad to introduce her to the local bank president so she could open her own accounts. She often mentioned her deeply held religious feelings and appeared to be very pious. I saw no reason to have another staff person double check all client receipts and bank deposits. I was about to learn the hard way about managing a business and its employees.

Monday morning finally arrived for me after a restless night of little sleep. I was at my office early and emptied Jean's desk, her family pictures, and her personal possessions into a box that sat ominously in the center of her now clear desk. I left a note on Jill's desk telling her I would be in a conference with Jean and not to interrupt us. She would know why when she saw Jean's cleared desk.

Jean walked in the door at exactly eight o'clock and walked to her desk, looked at the box and then walked into my office across the hallway with the face of a shocked, innocent child asked, "What is going on?" She stood there with her hands on her hips.

"Shut the door, Jean, and have a seat. We need to talk."

"You have been stealing money from me for months and now I have the proof I need, the only question is whether I will let you pay the money back or put you away in prison for felony embezzlement."

Jean's face turned white, then red, her chin started to tremble and her eyes brimmed with tears. "How can you say those things, I have never stolen a thing in my life!"

A hint of anger now in her voice. "I am a woman of God, and have never violated His Commandments!"

"Jean, do not play games with me; I have been watching you for weeks, and some of that cash you have been stealing were marked bills and traced to you and your bank account." I was trying to bluff her into a full confession; the tape-recorder in my desk was recording every word.

"Our CPA's audit confirmed that you have embezzled at least forty thousand dollars in cash over the last six months. If you lie to me - I will audit all the way back to when you started work here; so tell me the truth or I will call the police, right now!"

She wilted before my eyes, her shoulders slumped and her voice cracked, "My husband made me do it, I had no choice, he can't manage money, never could. I had to feed my family. I will pay back your money, just give me the chance and do not call the police. Please! He made me do it."

I handed her the document I had prepared and told her to read it and sign it. She scanned it and said, "I can't sign anything until I have my husband's consent, that is the Way of our Faith, I will bring it back signed tomorrow with as much money as I can obtain."

Her answer caught me by surprise and I said, "Okay, but you be back here at eight o'clock tomorrow morning or I will file criminal charges against you, understand?"

"Yes sir," she said meekly and walked away, picked up her box of items and walked out the front door without even looking at Jill's pale face.

I briefed Jill on what had occurred and she basically confirmed the information that Harriet had related. Jill was more direct in her opinion of Jean's real nature. "She is a damn hypocrite, worse I ever met, an' meaner than a junkyard dog!"

I told her to call the locksmith and change all office door-locks. I called our bank and told them Jean had been fired and no longer had any authority over our accounts.

Another anxious night passed slowly and at eight o'clock the next morning my office phone rang and I heard Jean's voice, which no longer had her usual sweetness attached to it, say coldly "Bob, I have left town, do not try to find me, and if you file criminal charges against me, *my friend* will come to your office and kill you!" Click. She hung up before I could utter a sound.

Jill walked into my office, "Was that Jean calling, her voice sounded different," she asked.

My thoughts were racing. "Jill, do you know where Jean and her family live and what do you know about Jean's boyfriend?"

Jill drew me a map to Jean's house. She told the same story as Harriet about Jean's boyfriend; big, tough looking, always in black and drove a truck, never talked to anyone but Jean. Jill had a frightened look on her face. "He always gave me the creeps."

"Jill, Jean just told me on the phone that if I file criminal charges on her she will have me killed, by *her friend*."

Harriet had now joined the conversation and her face was white and hands trembling. Both looked scared.

"Mr. Wilson, you need to call the police, she is dangerous, an evil woman." Jill nodded her head in agreement.

I smiled, "Oh, just relax, you two, she is just full of hot air and trying to scare me into not going after her. She does not scare me."

"But, keep a lookout for her boyfriend and if you see him walk in our front door, ring me immediately and stand ready to call the police, okay?"

The office phone rang and I picked it up to hear my wife's trembling voice, "Robert, how could you do those things to us?"

"What things?" I asked, trying to grasp the situation.

"Jean just called me and told me she had to quit, she could not stand coming into your office every Monday morning and clean up the mess you left on your desk and office floor. She said there were panties and used rubbers on the floor again this morning and she just could not work for such an evil man and wanted me to know what a monster I had married!"

I now discovered another error in judgment of mine; I had failed to inform my wife about Jean. They had become friends and I did not want to upset my wife, or possibly have her say something carelessly to someone which would have forewarned Jean of my intentions.

I told my wife as quickly as possible that I had proof that Jean had embezzled many thousands of dollars from us and I fired her when she came to work yesterday morning. That news just upset her more and I promised to tell her the full story later and that Jean was totally lying to her and she should have more faith in me than that, and hung up the phone.

A chill ran up my back. I was not dealing with a rational person, but a ruthless woman. I needed to watch my step, and my back.

I drove over to the address where Jean lived in an effort to find her and to talk to her husband to see if he knew what his wife had done and whether he was a co-conspirator in the money thefts.

I knocked on their door and no one responded. There was no vehicle present and the house was very quiet. I walked next door to ask the neighbor who was closely watching me if he had seen Jean or her husband that morning.

"Sister Jean and her family moved out last night, lock, stock, and barrel," the neighbor said in a calm voice like it was normal behavior.

I struggled to ask an intelligent question, my head spinning. "Where did they move?" was all I could manage.

"Said they had a family emergency and would send me a new address when they got wherever they were going, and asked me to buy their house for five thousand dollars cash which I did. I know a good bargain when I see one. Jean typed up an assumption warranty deed on the house last night and we had it notarized and everything and I am filing it at the recorder's office today. I bought all their household furnishings for five hundred dollars cash. Jean said her mother had a stroke and they needed money for her medical bills."

The neighbor could hardly believe his good luck with his recent purchases. "They only took their clothes and the whole family drove away late last night, I loaned them five hundred dollars for travel expenses, our church will miss them, he was our Pastor."

"Please let me know if you receive any word from them or a new address, it is very important that I speak to Jean," I said, knowing I was wasting my breath as I handed him my business card.

I felt like I had been outsmarted by Jean and realized I had made a mistake by allowing her the time to pack up and leave for parts unknown. I had hoped to recover some of my lost funds. I knew now I had no choice but to prosecute.

I returned to my office and informed Jill and Harriett of the news and went into my office to assemble the evidence I would need to file criminal charges.

Suddenly, Jill's shrill voice sounded over the intercom – "He just drove up in his truck, he's coming in and he is carrying *something* in his hand". My heart jumped into my throat, and without hesitation I hollered into the intercom for all to hear, "Both of you run into the back storage office and stay there until I tell you to come out. Harriet, call the police from the back phone and tell them we have a suspicious man in our office, and we need help." I reached into my office desk drawer and grabbed my fully loaded .357 revolver. "I guess Jean is not playing games," I said to myself as I walked out of my office toward the reception room in the front part of our office, my right hand tightly gripping the pistol I held behind my back.

I walked rapidly through the office hallway trying to meet this stranger at the front door. He was already walking through the doorway into the reception room.

He stood just inside the front door, looking around for someone, with a grim look on his face. He was exactly as described, both in appearance and dress. In his left hand he was holding a small paper sack and his right hand was in that sack, holding a pointed object. I assumed it was a weapon.

I brought my pistol around to my side so it was now clearly visible to him and shouted, "Freeze! What do you want?"

His face suddenly turned white and he stopped all motion. He looked at my pistol and the expression on my face and realized he had walked into a dangerous situation.

"I am looking for Jean, I brought her a coke," his voice had a pleading tone.

"Lay that sack down on the nearest chair and stand back," I said as I walked slowly toward him.

He quickly complied. The sack revealed a cold bottle of Coca-Cola, and nothing else.

"Did you know I fired Jean yesterday and she already moved out of town? Have you talked to her?" I demanded.

He seemed confused and perplexed, "No, I only returned last night, been on the road, and haven't talked to her."

Just then, two police cars pulled into our parking lot at high speed, with lights flashing. The stranger looked at them and at me, with fearful anticipation in his eyes. I placed the pistol in a desk drawer and asked the entering policemen to please check the stranger's identification and what business he had at our office. They took him outside into the parking lot and interviewed him, searched him, and checked for any wants or warrants.

One of the officers reported the man was there to see his *lady friend* and bring her a Coke and seemed to have no other purpose in mind. I told them to tell him he needed to stay away and he should not return, which they did, making sure he drove away first before they departed. The office was now empty and very quiet.

Wow, I thought, I almost shot an innocent man; my legs were trembling as I retrieved my pistol and walked to the back storage office to tell Jill and Harriet about the false alarm. They were trembling.

A phone call came an hour later from an investigator for a life insurance company trying to locate Jean's husband, their former salesman; it seems he disappeared without a trace several days ago, making no provision to repay several thousand dollars in missing insurance premiums he had collected from customers.

Later that day, Jean's neighbor, whom I talked to earlier, called and informed me that Sister Jean had cheated him. Jean failed to tell him her house was in foreclosure and when he advised the mortgage company that he now owned the house, they told him Jean was six months in arrears, which amount he would need to pay in full immediately if he wanted to keep that house. "I am beginning to suspect her of bad things," he moaned.

I decided not to prosecute Jean; I just wanted to forget I ever knew and trusted her so completely; I would not do that again. I just gave thanks the incident had not ended more tragically than it did. It could have been much worse.

Jean left no forwarding address. She never contacted any of her fellow church members or ever changed the address on her driver's license. Her two teenagers disappeared with her and were never formally checked out of their schools.

She and her family are wolves in sheep's clothing and are dangerous people. They are out there somewhere, undoubtedly ripping off trusting naïve people, so watch out. Her real full name is Jean Perkins, most likely still "*prayin' and stealin'*."

This expensive and stressful experience taught me to implement proper recordkeeping procedures for receiving and disbursing funds and verification of bank deposit preparation by at least two employees.

Only lawyers and painters can turn white to black.
Japanese Proverb

3

As word spread of my trial victories in both civil and criminal cases, my law practice started growing faster than I could expand my facilities and staff. Just about every type of potential client was now appearing in front of my desk asking for legal assistance - the young and old; the rich and poor; the sane and insane; and the good and bad.

The most important advice anyone can give a young lawyer, besides returning their clients' phone calls, is to be very careful about which clients and cases you accept because once you say "yes", you must follow through in providing professional services to that client, whether you want to or not.

One of the most bizarre cases to walk into my office was in the form of two highly educated, middle-aged engineers. They were well dressed and well-spoken and charged with felony malicious destruction of property, which carried a five to ten year prison sentence. I quoted them a very high fee thinking they would need time to discuss it and get back to me – and then disappear; client talk for "You charge too much."

I was mistaken. I was stunned when they wrote out a big check. I realized these guys expected a miracle and they both demanded a jury trial and outright acquittals.

I listened to their story of woe and had my doubts about their innocence. Tom and Jerry, my clients, were model plane builders and had organized a local flying club of model plane enthusiasts, which now numbered about thirty members. The club members were grown men, mostly in their thirties and forties and mostly well-educated and financially able to invest substantial sums into their hobby and spend almost every weekend working on and flying their planes.

These were not small planes; some of them had wingspans of twelve feet or more with powerful hi-tech engines with ear-splitting noise levels. My impression of the hobby was that it was recreational flying for men who never grew up.

I learned from my clients that there were several flying clubs such as theirs in the Dallas-Fort Worth area and the clubs were super-competitive with each other and bad blood existed between some clubs. It reminded me of high school drama between jealous girls. My clients' club, the Spitfires, had angered another flying club by stealing away some of its members and things recently had reached a boiling point.

One club hostile to the Spitfires always used a certain abandoned commercial parking lot as their flying field that was near a lake and each Sunday they practiced takeoffs and landings with their planes.

On one particular Sunday, while six of that club's valuable planes were in flight over the lake and under control of their owners' transmitters and instruments, all six planes' engines suddenly stopped in midair and they nosedived into the lake and sank – to be lost forever.

The frustrated and very angry flying club members jumped into their cars and began an extensive search of the immediate area looking for any possible culprits. Several club members observed my two clients sitting quietly in their car near the lake. They called the Tarrant County sheriff's office and a deputy responded promptly and was directed to question my two clients.

Several of the angry club members and the deputy sheriff looked into my clients' vehicle, which was a convertible with the top down. In the back seat, on the floorboard in plain sight, was a black box about the size of a shoebox. The device had dials and electronic gauges on it and when the deputy asked my clients what the device was, they replied coolly "It's just a controller box for one of our model airplanes."

The deputy seized the device at the urging of the flying club members who had now gathered around the suspects, and the deputy arrested my two clients when they were unable to explain why they were in the area at that time. "Just taking a Sunday drive," was not a sufficient excuse.

The lost planes had a value well over two thousand dollars and even more important – one of the club's victims was a close relative of the local district attorney. My new clients' felony charges had been placed on the fast track for trial and several months later a jury trial date was set with two of county's best felony prosecutors assigned to the case. The prosecutor's plea deal of two years in prison for each defendant, with full restitution, was quickly rejected.

The pressure was on and everyone knew it. When I walked out of the Tarrant County Courthouse after a pre-trial hearing on the case, the entire rival flying club membership was waiting for me next to my parked car. Several of them had put on their leather motorcycle jackets and were carrying short chains for emphasis.

They shouted in unison: "How can you represent such scum? Better watch your back!"

I smiled and waved and quickly drove away wondering what I had gotten myself involved in.

I knew nothing about the flying of, or the construction of, these model planes – but I needed to know more than the prosecutors if I intended to walk my clients out of that courtroom as free men. My clients had treated me to a thick instructor's manual on the subject at hand, which explained the finer points of the construction, power plants, electronic controls and operation of these planes. I also researched who was considered the top expert in the field of electronics of these large flying models.

The gentleman who was considered the father of modern model plane flying was also the publisher of the top selling model flying magazine in the country – I called him.

"Can't talk to you," was his immediate reply – "I have already been retained by the state to testify for the state at your clients' trial, and by the way – "*they are dead meat.*"

"Wonderful," I thought. The phone conversation was somewhat unsettling – so I called several other gentlemen around the country who were recognized experts in the electronic control of model flying airplanes. They had all heard about the case since it was now national news in the flying model industry and they all hoped my clients would be "strung up on the courthouse lawn." I could find no expert willing to testify on behalf of my clients.

I studied the model plane electronics manual diligently, to the point of keeping it by my nightstand as a sleep aid. I knew that if you wanted to be a trial lawyer who wins more cases than you lose, you must know more that your opposing counsel about the subject matter at hand. You need to be able to absorb vast amounts of information and keep it fresh in your mind so that in an instant you can recall it to challenge a witness's testimony – or completely discredit the witness in front of the jury by catching them in a falsehood. A jury who discovers a witness has lied to them under oath will discard that witness's opinions whether he or she is an expert or a lay witness.

The trial jury began. The state's prima-facie case was made quickly by the testimony of the hostile flying club members and the arresting deputy sheriff. The star prosecution witness would be their last witness – the publisher and model plane expert. The courtroom was packed, the benches on one side were my clients' backers and family; on the other side the benches were packed with all the hostile flying club members and family. Of course, a few local news reporters were present as well.

The trial had a carnival-like atmosphere, with cheers erupting from one side or the other side of the courtroom, depending on whether the witness had just hurt or helped the team of hard charging prosecutors or myself, the one young defense attorney who was constantly referring to his stack of model airplane manuals on his counsel table.

The easy going judge finally lost his chess playing patience – finally banging his gavel loudly enough to wake the dead, "I will clear the courtroom unless everyone stops this behavior, one more outburst or cheer and it's all over." The courtroom suddenly was very quiet and stayed that way for the duration, since no one in the audience wanted to miss a single word of testimony.

I knew I would have to call my clients as witnesses and even though they had clean records and awesome education and employment histories – they were arrogant smart asses and no matter how I cautioned them about their need to show humility in front of the jury – they were so devoid of empathy they scared me to death.

I had no good excuse as to why they were less than one-half mile away from the disaster area when the planes went down. Furthermore, their possession of a black electronic box without a model plane with them was a big problem. The state's expert was surely going to describe in his testimony that my clients were in possession of what is called a *crash box* – only capable of jamming the controls of any flying model plane within a one-mile radius.

The state's expert proudly took the witness stand as their last witness – their cleanup hitter. The courtroom grew apprehensive and very quiet. His credentials were impressive. He and his publication had almost single-handedly built the national craze for large flying model planes.

Mr. Expert spent an hour talking about his expertise and experience while I sat back and let him talk. The judge glared at me and tried to mentally force me to stipulate to his expertise in the field. I watched the jury's eyes starting to glaze over and close after they had just returned from their lunch hour, a few even drifted off and their neighbors elbowed them awake.

Finally after everyone was beginning to have distaste for the expert's boring and technical evidence – the prosecutor finally popped the big question.

"Sir, have you examined in detail the State's Exhibit #12, the black box of electronics that was found in those defendants' vehicle?" The prosecutor pointed at the two stone-faced defendants.

"Yes sir, I have."

"What is your expert opinion as to the use of that device?"

"It is a called a crash-box and made solely for the purpose of jamming the controls of any flying model planes within a certain radius of that box." The expert turned to the jury and smiled – his work completed.

The witness was passed.

I jumped up from my table to get everyone's attention and loudly asked: "Mr. Expert, did I understand you to testify here, under oath, that the only purpose this black box has is to jam the controls of any flying model planes within a certain area?"

"Yes, sir it is my expert opinion, that black box was built only for that purpose." He turned and smiled again at the jury.

I walked over to the jury box and turned to the witness – "So, if I understand you, I can't use this black box to fly one of those large model planes?"

"That's right, it has no *useful* purpose."

"You would stake your reputation on that?" I asked pointing my finger at him.

"Yes sir," he replied with a confident smile.

"Pass the witness." Everyone, including my clients, was puzzled and concerned about my limited cross-examination of the state's star witness.

The state rested its case and I asked the judge: "Can we take a fifteen minute break while my clients go out to their truck and bring up a heavy item of evidence?" The two prosecutors looked alarmed but said nothing, and the judge announced the afternoon breaks.

When court resumed, my clients and I were not seated at our usual counsel table; we stood behind the railing because there was only room on our counsel table for the large model plane, with its twelve foot wide wingspread that now was the center of attention in the courtroom.

The judge's eyes were wide and his face stern when he took his seat. He looked at the plane and then me – "Mr. Wilson, what's going on?"

"Your honor, I need the court reporter to mark this plane as an exhibit, call it defense exhibit #14." The judge rolled his eyes and motioned to the prosecutors and me, "Approach the bench, gentlemen."

The judge continued outside the hearing of the jury. "Wilson, what the hell are you up to?" he asked sharply. He had a reputation as a fair but stern, no nonsense judge.

"Judge, I am going to call my clients to the stand and have them fly this plane around this courtroom with that black box the prosecution placed in evidence. The state has based their entire case on their evidence that that box can only be used to jam controls, nothing else."

"You will not fly that plane in my courtroom!" The judge's voice made that point clear to all.

"O.K. Judge, but I request this court and jury go outside and watch while my clients fly that plane up and down the street with that black box that the state has put in evidence with great fanfare and testimony about its only use is to jam controls."

The judge turned to the state's attorney, "He's right, men. Your expert says that box only has one function – if these defendants can fly that plane, this trial is over with – I may even direct an acquittal." The judge was looking sternly at the prosecutors – who had lost their smiles.

I spoke up in an effort to solve the dilemma. "Judge, I will compromise and agree to not fly the plane in the courtroom or outside – just let us start the engine and control the movement of that plane's rudders and other gadgets on the plane with that box in evidence and I will not demand the plane be actually flown."

Everyone agreed to that compromise.

I called the less abrasive of my two clients to the stand and asked him if he and his co-defendant had done anything to cause the other flying club planes to crash or malfunction the day in question.

"No sir, we were only watching them fly their planes from across the lake, we did nothing to harm their planes."

"Was that black box in your car for any particular reason?" I asked.

"No, I had left it in the car from our last flying event. I use it to fly my plane." The jury exchanged looks of surprise at that response.

"Can you fly this plane that is here in this courtroom with that black box that has been admitted into evidence?" I asked Tom, as I handed him the state's exhibit black box.

"Yes sir, I sure can."

"Please start the engine of your plane and operate the controls on the wings and tail, but do not cause it to take off and fly," I instructed and held my breath.

Tom turned dials and made adjustments to the back box and suddenly the plane's engines sputtered and caught and made everyone jump almost out of their seats from the high-pitched whine. Soon the engine was running smoothly and loud. Everyone covered their ears. The prosecutors exchanged looks of horror.

Above the noise, I shouted, "Now use your controls."

Suddenly the plane's rudder and ailerons were moving smoothly up and down as my other client and I firmly held onto the surging plane – because it obviously wanted to fly away.

Then for good measure, Tom started to remotely race the engine up and down until the courthouse was now echoing and vibrating from the ear-splitting noise. Court bailiffs poured into the courtroom, their hands on their side arms.

The judge screamed at the witness – "Turn that thing off – now," which he did remotely from the witness stand.

The courtroom was now standing room only. Every courthouse employee and visitor who could squeeze into the courtroom was now watching the circus.

When everything quieted down the judge looked at me, "Mr. Wilson, do you rest?" Which was his way of saying the trial was over. I had only called one witness.

"Yes sir, we rest."

The state had no rebuttal witnesses.

The judge turned to the jury, "The evidence is finished and tomorrow morning the lawyers' will give their closing arguments to you – be back at nine o'clock in the morning – do not discuss this case with anyone.

Court adjourned and the jury filed out – the judge looked over at the two quiet prosecutors and slowly shook his head without saying a word – we knew what he was going to do – let the case go to the jury so as to not embarrass the D.A.'s office with a directed verdict of acquittal – but if the jury didn't acquit the defendants, he would do so later with a bench ruling in favor of a defense motion to disregard the jury's verdict.

The next day the jury returned with smiles for all and a verdict before noon – both defendants were fully acquitted and returned to their normal lives and their Spitfire companions.

My clients shook my hand after court was adjourned. "See, we told you we were innocent – they were just trying to frame us."

I cautioned them about pushing their luck and suggested they stay away from the other flying clubs airfields. They shrugged and walked away, never to be heard from again.

Years later, the local major newspaper interviewed the retiring trial judge who had served almost thirty years on the criminal trial bench. Their reporter asked him – "Judge, of the thousands of criminal trials you have presided over, which case comes to mind as the most unusual or bizarre?"

His immediate response, "The case that comes to my mind is the model airplane case when a young defense lawyer wanted to fly a huge model plane around in my courtroom."

Litigation: A machine you go into as a pig and come out of as a sausage.
The Devil's Dictionary

4

THE THREE YEARS OF REQUIRED LAW SCHOOL for lawyers has one overriding purpose – and it is not to teach law – that is a necessary byproduct. The real purpose of reading and discussing thousands of pages of old case law is to train the student's mind to think like a lawyer. In other words, learn to digest a mind numbing set of convoluted, confusing facts and from that pit of confusion be able to clearly state a list of legal issues. Then arrange those facts in such a manner as to create a cause of action or remedy for the benefit of your client.

A seasoned lawyer soon learns, usually the hard way – that other important factors must be taken into consideration before accepting a case - those factors are not taught in law school. These can include the character of your clients, the potential defendants, the probable defendants' legal counsel, and most important – who is going to be the judge. Of course, the financial strength of each party is of the utmost importance as well. Litigation can be very expensive and time consuming.

A lawyer must ask himself: is the blood, sweat, expense, and tears to be encountered worth the final cost in money and time? Keeping in mind at all times – there is no prize for second place in litigation. The final outcome of a complex lawsuit can take years to achieve and everyone's patience is sure to be exhausted by that time and in the final analysis – was it really worth it?

I too, had to learn the hard way.

Alfred, a mild mannered and obviously honest and intent fellow presented himself one morning, asking me to solve a matter of great concern for him. He had been referred to me by one of the leading lawyers in the area who had told him bluntly – "There is only one lawyer in the county who has the guts and ambition to take on your case – Bob Wilson."

At first glance, the facts appeared fairly simple – but this matter would be anything but simple for all concerned. Alfred set the stage for what was to become one of my most difficult and remarkable cases. I would not know or understand the full ramifications of this case until after the several years it took to litigate the mess.

Alfred and his business partner, Roy, had been childhood friends. They grew up to become best buddies and opened a successful appliance store which did well for several years and their banker suggested they should expand with a second store which the bank would be happy to finance and provide an inventory line of credit.

Their first store was an incorporated business, with each partner owning one-half of the company's issued stock. They had selected a great location for their second store and with their bank's liberal financing – they soon had the new store open and operating. Their bank insisted they form a new corporation to own the second store and that the two men should each own one-half of that second company's issued common stock.

Each partner had signed a personal guarantee of all debt owed to the bank by both companies. The bank also required that the new store use the same CPA that handled the bank's accounts.

Everything seemed to be going well for a year or so, until one day a former employee of the second store called Alfred and told him "Something fishy is going on with that bank and Roy – you better get a lawyer before you get cheated."

Alfred was shocked and deeply hurt by the employee's warning and had not spoken to anyone but his wife Karen about that conversation or his own fears. Alfred had not been able to work or sleep since.

Jimmy, the former employee of store number two, had quit his job because he suspected something illegal was going on. "He was not going to be part of it," Alfred said.

"So what does Jimmy say is the big problem?" I asked.

"Counting empty boxes," Alfred answered expecting me to see the problem immediately.

"What empty boxes?" I asked – hoping for clarification.

"Empty appliance boxes – you know refrigerators, gas ranges, hot water heaters – you know – they all come in big boxes with their serial numbers on the boxes."

"Why would anyone want to count empty boxes?" I inquired.

"That's what I wanted to know. Jimmy says he is not a trouble maker and he will not tell me anything else – will only speak to my lawyer about what he knows – so, I want to hire you to talk to Jimmy and do a full investigation because Jimmy says I am being screwed by my partner *and* the bank."

I heard the stress in Alfred's voice and could clearly see the circles under his eyes from lack of sleep. I wondered out loud why the other lawyer had declined representation.

"Why did the other attorney say he would not represent you," I asked.

"I think he is scared of the bank and its resources – it is very active in local politics," Alfred replied.

There was much truth to his statement – large banks in small counties carried a lot of weight, both financially and politically. Having represented several local banks on routine matters I doubted a bank would do anything to damage its reputation or their own loan collateral. I suggested this was probably much to do over very little. I could not have been more mistaken. I agreed to look into the matter for Alfred and he signed a retainer agreement and the legal ride of my life was about to start.

I called Jimmy and made an appointment to meet him at his house. He readily agreed and then volunteered – "There are two other former store employees that you need to interview as well. Do you want me to bring them to my house when you are here?" he asked.

I felt a sudden uneasiness run through my body. This really might be a serious matter after all.

"Yes, have everyone there that is willing to talk to me about what is going on in that store."

As soon as Jimmy was off the phone I called a court reporter and asked her to come with me to the meeting and bring her equipment, "We may be there for a while taking sworn statements."

I interviewed and took four sworn statements from three former employees of store number two and one customer of that store who was Jimmy's friend.

The stories they told were all verified by each other and could only lead to one rational conclusion – *bank fraud* – on a grand scale, with some sex and adultery thrown in.

Roy managed store number two, but Alfred owned one-half of that company's stock – but his only clue to that store's financial health was its monthly profit and loss statements supplied by the company's CPA. The past profit and loss statements showed no cause for alarm and that everything was rosy.

The sworn statements I took indicated that those profit and loss statements had to be false and store number two was actually losing money on a grand scale. What shocked me most was that the bank and its auditors were covering up the losses by padding their own records and allowing Roy to operate his store on borrowed bank funds while the store's inventory was being sold without reduction of that store's corresponding bank debt.

My witnesses' statements revealed that whenever a large appliance was sold by the store – it was delivered to the customer and the box or container was returned to the store and placed back with the existing inventory boxes. When the bank auditors came once a month to do a floor-plan inventory of its collateral – the empty boxes were counted as well as the unsold boxes of expensive appliances. The proper procedure was for store number two to pay the bank each time one of the appliances was sold, but that was not being done.

The witnesses had even seen the bank's auditors kick the empty boxes and laugh as they counted them. The end result was large sums of money were not being accounted for and a fake inventory was being created to cover for the missing funds.

"But why would the bank want to cover up losses for the store, it's the bank's money that is disappearing?" I asked.

"There is something going on between those bankers and Roy and his wife – we have seen that bank president and his top vice president drinking and making-out with Roy's wife, right in front of Roy – and he just laughs it off. Roy is a hopeless drunk and likes the good life the bank is providing."

"Wow," I said out loud.

"How am I going to prove the bank's president and vice president are having sex with Roy's wife and he goes along with it?" I asked.

"I saw them," Jimmy replied. "They were all out on the lake in Roy's new inboard cruiser and I went along as a deck hand. Roy and his wife were tooted and the bank president and his vice president took turns doing Roy's wife in the boat's bedroom. Roy was so drunk he didn't seem to care what she did with those bankers."

"Why would the bank's auditors cover-up the missing inventory, it just doesn't make sense?" I asked all of them.

Jimmy spoke first – "It only makes sense if you know Alfred has personally guaranteed all those bank notes and when the time arrives – and the partying is over, the bank is going to call upon him to cover that entire missing inventory. They will let Roy and his wife off the hook and screw Alfred but good, and he will have to cover all those bank loans out of his pocket."

I did not say anything but thought Jimmy was probably right – sometime in the future, there was going to be a big bang and Alfred, the frugal and honest partner was going to be the big loser. Roy and his wife and the bank president and his vice president had so much dirt on each other they would have to put up a solid wall of lies and protect each other and dump all the liability in Alfred's lap at some time in the future.

I assembled all my investigation facts and met with Alfred – who was maddened and saddened by my report.

"I just want out of this partnership. Roy can have his store and the bank's indebtedness. I just want my store and a release of my guarantee with the bank. We can then go our separate ways, peacefully."

Alfred owed nothing to the bank on the store he managed. But, he owned one-half the stock of both stores, so life just got complicated. It was going to be difficult to talk Roy into giving up his interest in the profitable store and end up with the insolvent store and face all its unpaid debt at the bank.

"Will you speak to the bank on my behalf and see if a quiet settlement can be worked out?" Alfred asked. I agreed that was the best course of action, but not easy to achieve.

"I suspect it will be a bumpy ride from this point on once Roy and the bank realize the fun and games are over," I said.

The next day I called the bank president and told him I wanted a meeting with him and his board of directors. His voice quivered when I explained very briefly what I suspected had been going on between the bank and store number two. He agreed to a time and date for a meeting in his bank's boardroom.

I arrived at the bank at the appointed time with my briefcase, copies of the witness statements and a release of Alfred's guarantee. I also offered a smiling face and an extended hand of friendship to all.

I was ushered into the boardroom. No other directors were present, only the bank president, the suspect vice president and three lawyers – all five men wearing grim faces. One lawyer did all the talking – he was the former president of the local bar association and a legal bigwig.

He introduced himself as speaking on behalf of the bank and his next words were, "Are you trying to blackmail this bank? This is the largest bank in the county and if you say or do anything to damage its reputation – we will cut off your head and hand it to you."

I looked into the deadpan eyes of the president and vice president and there was no response shown to their counsel's statement. I turned on my heels and walked back out the door and said loud enough for all in the bank to hear - "See all you folks in court!"

Events moved fast over the next several days at my direction – a fraud and conspiracy case was filed against the bank, its two officers, and Roy and his wife as co-conspirators to commit fraud. A forensic auditor was hired to audit the financial books of store number two. A private investigator was retained to dig up evidence about the juicy relationship between Roy, his wife and the two bank executives. I filed an official death threat complaint concerning the bank's counsel's statement – including a copy sent to the entire board of directors of the bank.

I took depositions from Roy and his wife. Roy had a problem explaining how he paid cash for his expensive new boat and how he and his wife could afford an expensive home in an exclusive neighborhood – while his equal partner, Alfred and his wife lived in a much more modest home, with no boat or lavish lifestyle.

As the case gathered steam and headed toward a jury trial conclusion – it became discussed far and wide by the locals. Two other local banks hired me on minor cases and one bank put my office on retainer. They did not want to worry about any of their unhappy loan customers hiring that *Wilson guy* to sue them.

The private investigator we hired confirmed there was certainly a *sex and loans* relationship going on between Roy and his wife and the two top bank officers. It was difficult to determine who was taking advantage of whom. Roy's wife was giving up her favors freely in exchange for a lifestyle furnished by the bank and its cooked books. The audit of the store's records revealed approximately two hundred thousand dollars in missing inventory that no one could explain.

The legal issues became even more complicated when Roy and the bank tried to roadblock a trial by claiming Roy and Alfred were equal shareholders in both stores and whatever legally happened to one partner, also had to happen to the other. Their contention was that a total and complete deadlock in both corporations had occurred and Alfred did not have the legal authority to sue on behalf of either of the two corporations. In other words, neither partner was a majority shareholder, so neither had complete control of either corporation and therefore, neither had authority to sue on behalf of either corporation. After all, who was really being damaged, corporation number two - or, its two shareholders? How was Alfred personally being damaged? It was a legal nightmare. One of my cardinal rules of business advice was to become: Do not have an equal ownership in a partnership or corporation between two persons since it almost guarantees a total deadlock in corporate or partnership affairs if problems arise between the two equal partners – not unlike a marriage and divorce.

The bank started pulling its political strings at the courthouse and the trial date kept being delayed and postponed. Finally, the case went to trial after much legal hair pulling and stalling. Several days of wild testimony followed from the witness stand as two bankers tried desperately to keep their jobs and cover their asses. It didn't work. The trial lasted sixteen days and many witnesses testified. After closing arguments the jury returned in short order with a verdict in favor of Alfred and his corporation for several hundred thousand dollars against the bank and his former partner.

The political judge refused to sign the judgment against the bank, using various excuses and delays. Eleven months passed with no judgment signed and no further bank financing of corporation number two. The bank called in all its political markers. The second corporation was forced to file bankruptcy proceedings to try to preserve its remaining assets. Only then did the judge sign the judgment. It was immediately appealed to the court of appeals by the bank.

The bank board fired its president, the vice president, and its smart-mouth lawyer that had got them into the smelly mess. Another local bank elected me to their board of directors – "keep your enemies closer" – as the saying goes.

One year later my client's money judgment was reversed on appeal due to technical issues caused by the unjust delay in securing a final judgment and the subsequent bankruptcy proceedings. The case was later re-tried by all before a different judge and jury - and the new judge did not put up with any bank nonsense and signed the new four hundred fifty thousand dollar judgment in Alfred's favor within a few days of the second jury's verdict being returned. The bank immediately appealed. Again, the court of appeals reversed the judgment on technical grounds.

My client called me shortly before the second judgment was reversed - and said that he had seen one of the three appellate judges whose court was reviewing the judgment in the subject bank doing loan business. I immediately filed a motion for that appellate judge to recuse himself from being one of the reviewing judges. He refused to recuse himself and that court promptly reversed the judgment on technical grounds – and, this time, ruled the case could not be re-tried again.

Politics had carried the day. Over three years of difficult legal toil came to nothing. My client was almost broke and I had invested heavily myself in the case and even though we won two long jury trials and much respect in the community – neither of us really won anything. But, no banker ever looked at me the same way thereafter, and even though I was to serve on two different boards of directors of state and national banks in the future – I still have a bitter taste in my mouth for bankers and their kind for the way they use their banks' money to gain power and coercion over their hapless loan customers.

My client did finally obtain sole ownership of his store, without further bank interference. His former partner and his wife left town. The two fired bankers moved to another city and opened a new bank.

By law, state and national bank regulations clearly demand that banks must serve the needs of the local citizens in the area those banks have offices or branches. However, I witnessed firsthand that as the local banks were forced by the bank regulators to be acquired by large national banks – little money was loaned for local projects – customer's deposits flowed to the purchase of federal securities or to other national banks in exchange for participation in huge multi-national loans that were of no benefit to the local communities or citizens. Many of those huge participation loans were to foreign countries to be later written off as losses.

LAWFUL, adj.
Compatible with the will of a judge having jurisdiction.
The Devil's Dictionary

5

ONE MORNING, A LARGE HISPANIC FAMILY GREETED me when I arrived at my office, La Madre and her seven children ranging in age from seven to seventeen. El Padre was in the Hill County jail, charged with capital murder – with no bail possible. According to the wife and oldest daughter's story, related in a mixture of English and Spanish, the family Patron was falsely charged with shooting and robbing a man, in front of several eyewitnesses. The wife and children all swore; "Padre was home with us when the stranger was shot – our padre was *an innocent man and being framed*."

The family had scraped together several thousand dollars working in the cotton fields and did not want the court-appointed lawyer to defend padre, they wanted me – because: "I was *a good lawyer who got his client justice*."

I explained to deaf ears that they couldn't afford to hire me and that they needed to let the court-appointed counsel represent their padre. They persisted and argued until the oldest daughter, Angelica, a very attractive young teenager, said she would "work free at my office for one year if I would defend her padre." She impressed me as a young woman who was very bright and had complete faith in her father. Any father would have been very proud to have such a daughter. Her offer to work caught my interest, I needed to hire a new file clerk and her offer was enough to change my mind. I agreed to take the case, probably another money loser, but an interesting case.

I asked Angelica and her mother to meet me at the scene of the shooting the following weekend. I needed to see the crime scene before I made a decision. At that time the three of us met at the county road bridge under which the shooting occurred. I walked from the paved roadway down into the flowing creek bed under the bridge. It was full of empty beer cans and broken wine bottles. This secluded location was obviously a frequent drinking hole for migrant farm workers in the area. Some serious drinking and partying occurred under that bridge. What really caught my attention were the many empty metal cartridge shells of various calibers scattered about. Drinking and firearms are a dangerous combination – someone could get shot.

I had obtained copies of the sheriff's incident reports on the shooting. "A Hispanic male was shot to death and was DOA at the local hospital. A large group of local farm workers scattered after the shooting and no one stayed to be interviewed."

As we walked around under the bridge my clients talked: "Padre was not well liked by the other farm workers because he owned his own farm and never hired *outside* workers. The dead man was a heavy drinker and carried large sums of cash – which he bragged about to anyone who would listen. His luck finally run out and someone shot and robbed him."

I filed the usual discovery motions. One motion I filed expressly requested copies of the county's medical examiner's report and any x-rays taken of the body of the deceased victim. I soon received copies of everything I demanded, with the exception of the autopsy report and the body x-rays. I called the D.A.'s office and was told "We can't find those items, we are still looking and will send them to you as soon as they are located." That never happened.

I suspected a cover-up of some nature was taking place and was concerned the prosecutor's office was attempting to hide evidence that contradicted the state's theory: that Jesús (El Padre) had shot and robbed the deceased. A court-appointed attorney, whose pay came from the county with the judge's approval, was not likely to accuse the prosecutor of hiding exculpatory evidence.

No weapon was ever found and no physical evidence could be linked to Jesús. The indictment alleged "Jesús did intentionally and knowingly shoot the deceased one time causing his death with a .22 caliber pistol with the intent to kill and rob him of money." The state must prove each and every element of their indictment for a conviction to be upheld.

Jesús was also charged with robbery and assault with a deadly weapon. A conviction of murder and armed robbery would make the case a capital case, meaning death or a mandatory life sentence. My client was in a no-bail situation in the county jail so I pushed the matter to trial. The only plea bargain offer from the D.A. was twenty years in prison, which the client and his family soundly rejected.

Jesús was a small man, probably no more than one hundred and twenty pounds and stood about five foot five. His wife was a large woman, twice his weight. You had to wonder how a man and wife eating the same meals over many years of marriage could end up with such a weight difference. Probably hard physical work on his farm made for the difference.

The trial date arrived and I still had not been provided with the M.E.'s report and x-rays. It was now crunch time and I sent my female investigator with a subpoena to the Dallas county medical examiner's office where the autopsy had been performed and subpoenaed the M.E. himself and his report and his x-rays. He was mad as an old wet hen. He sat glaring out of the door of the courthouse witness room. I had briefed my investigator earlier to tell the M.E. that we had to subpoena him because the local D.A. would not produce a copy of his autopsy report – that way the M.E. would be equally mad at both the D.A. and me.

I watched the prosecutor's face when he saw the M.E. walk into courthouse witness room. His face alternated between red and white, he glanced over at me but avoided eye contact - I had hit a nerve. There was something really wrong about this case. I just needed to put my finger on it and bring it to the court or jury's attention before it was too late. I did not expect much sympathy from the judge, a former prosecutor, or the jury that was seated, an all-white collection of farmers, ranchers and housewives. They were good God-fearing folks who had no use for drinking, partying or "Mex'cins."

A locally elected prosecutor in a small farming and ranching community lives or dies by his reputation for enforcing law and order for its citizens. A district attorney's oath is to *see that justice is done* – which translates in real life to mean to "get convictions at all costs or face an opponent in the next election."

The picturesque courthouse of white limestone looked like a Norman Rockwell painting, peaceful and warm. Willie Nelson had seen its interior several times on marijuana charges. But, he had also entertained the locals with a concert on the courthouse grounds and had been forgiven for his trespasses.

The old cigar-chomping judge called the court to order on the first day of trial and promised the jurors, "We will finish the trial quickly so you folks can return to your families and farms" – he then looked at me and said, "Understand something gentlemen, no stalling, keep it movin'," I smiled and nodded in agreement.

The prosecutor's opening argument was short and to the point.

"We will prove the defendant, Jesús, shot the deceased in cold blood and robbed him of his money." I waived opening argument until later.

The state's first witness was a large Hispanic woman who testified she was sitting in a folding chair, under the bridge drinking a *coke* when; "I heard men arguing about fifty feet away and heard a gunshot and saw a man grab his stomach and fall to the ground." Then without the usual prompting from the state; she pointed at Jesús sitting meekly next to me, "He is the man I saw standing with a gun in his hand that night."

The D.A. walked over and stood behind Jesús and pointed down at the top of his head – "Are you sure this is the man you saw holding a gun?"

"Yes sir, he was holding a small gun and walked over and put his hands into the poor dead man's pants and just walked away into the darkness like nothin' happened."

The D.A. walked back to the witness and asked, "What did you do?"

"I screamed and ran to my car and drove home." The witness was passed.

I walked up to the witness, making sure I blocked the witness from the view of the prosecutor.

"Maria – can I call you Maria?"

"Sí, I mean yes, everyone else does."

"What time of night was it when you heard that shot?"

"About eleven thirty," she replied, her voice starting to quiver slightly.

"It was pitch black darkness under that bridge wasn't it?" I asked.

"We had campfires burning – there was light from the fires," she replied.

"How many men were gathered around those fires?"

"Twenty or so, I don't know for sure."

"Did you know all their names?" I asked.

Maria tried to look around me at the D.A. but I moved to block her view.

"Nada – I mean no – I only knew a few names," she replied.

"Did you know that man's name?" I asked and pointed at Jesús.

"Nada – I mean no," was her faint reply.

"Have you ever seen him before that night when you say you saw him holding a gun?"

"Nada – I mean no, I had never seen him before that night."

"Were you drinking that night?" I asked, as I walked over toward the jury – which meant she had to now face the jury.

"Nada – only a coke," she quickly said.

"Was everyone else drinking beer or wine?"

She looked over at the prosecutor who stared down at his notes.

"Sí, I think so," she smiled.

"So you were the only person there that night not drinking beer or wine?" I asked with raised eyebrows watching for the jury's reaction to her next words.

"Sí, I only drink coke."

"Why were you even there that night?" I asked.

Maria was starting to look very uncomfortable and uneasy. The prosecutor was on his feet, "Objection – counsel is badgering the witness."

"Let's move on gentlemen," the judge's voice showing his impatience.

"What did the other men do after the gunshot?" I asked.

"They all ran to their cars and left, like me," she replied.

"Who called the sheriff or ambulance," I asked.

"No se, I mean – I don't know, I was too afraid to do anything."

"Maria – did you have your glasses on when you heard that gunshot?" I asked. I had noticed Maria's new glasses and she seemed uncomfortable with them. Maria looked at the prosecutor, the judge and then back at me.

"No I couldn't afford to wear glasses then."

A stir and murmur swept through the numerous courtroom spectators and the twelve jurors.

I moved in for the kill. "Maria isn't it true you have to wear glasses to see clearly and you are restricted to only driving your car with your glasses on?" I had earlier checked out her Texas driver's license information.

Pure panic ran across Maria's face, she looked helplessly at the judge. She did not answer my question. I stood and walked over toward the jury and asked, "When did you buy those glasses you have on today?"

"About a month ago," she replied.

"Please take off your glasses for a moment," I instructed.

"Objection – he is badgering the witness again," the prosecutor was on his feet.

"Mr. Wilson, are these questions necessary?" The judge's impatient voice inquired.

"Yes, your honor, Maria said she saw my client that night from a distance of fifty feet and I want to see if she is believable."

"Let's move on gentlemen – what is your question for this witness?" the judge asked.

Maria removed her glasses and I asked, "Maria – sitting exactly fifty feet in front of you in the center of this courtroom's benches in the back of this well-lit courtroom sits my investigator. Please tell this jury if that person is a man or a woman?" I turned and pointed to the blonde, well-dressed woman who was my investigator. She smiled in return from her seat exactly fifty feet from where the witness sat. All twelve pairs of juror's eyes were now watching the witness as she squinted her eyes and struggled to focus on my investigator's appearance.

"I can only tell you it is a brown-headed person, can't say if it's a man or woman," was Maria's weak defeated reply.

I passed the witness and all twelve pairs of juror's eyes were now directed at the prosecutor who avoided their eyes and called his next eyewitness, José.

José was an older man who worked at various local farms doing manual labor. He was well-known and nearing retirement age. He could not speak English, according to him.

A court approved interpreter was required and could be counted on to create a circus atmosphere in the courtroom as my client's family was sure to dispute the coming testimony from José. After a local lady interpreter had been questioned by the court and shown to be unbiased and competent for the court's appointment, José took the stand, with the lady interpreter sitting next to him.

The prosecutor instructed the interpreter: "Tell this jury what you saw that night a man was shot." The D.A.'s voice was louder than normal, trying to show confidence and enjoying his opportunity to now blatantly lead his witness because of the use of the interpreter.

The interpreter answered with: "A bunch of workers were gathered around two campfires – eating and drinking. I was only there because my sons needed me to drive them. They don't have cars or drivers' licenses. All of a sudden I heard arguing and looked over at a group of men and there was a gunshot. I saw that man over there holding a gun. Everyone ran away, including me."

A tap on my shoulder from the oldest daughter confirmed my fears of what was coming. "That's not what *he* said". Everyone in the courtroom heard the teenage girl's whispered comment.

I took advantage of the judge's look of concern and rose to my feet. "Can this young lady sit next to me and assist with the interpretation of this witness' testimony; I cannot speak or understand Spanish". The judge gave his half-hearted consent.

José's testimony had him pointing at Jesús and then looking over at the jury and smiling. Again, my new assistant whispered for all to hear: "The witness did not say that, the interpreter is lying!" A loud murmur rose from the back of the courtroom from my client's family members: "She's right – that witness did not say that!"

The judge was losing his cool demeanor and ordered: "Mr. Bailiff, take the jury to their room, we need to clear up some matters before we can continue."

The judge looked at me and at the prosecutor, "Gentlemen, this cannot continue, the jury will have to decide what this witness is saying."

The judge called the lawyers to his bench, "Mr. Wilson, bring *that girl* with you."

"Young lady, you are disrupting my courtroom. That has to stop – you hear me?"

Without a moment's hesitation came her sharp reply, "My Padre is on trial for murder and *that woman* over there is not telling this jury what José is really sayin', I can't sit here and listen to her lyin'!"

"So what do you say that the witness said," the judge asked.

"He said my padre *looks like* the shooter; he did not say he *is the shooter.*"

The judge looked over at the interpreter, "So Ma'am, which is it? Did the witness say that this defendant is the shooter or he looks like the shooter?" The woman's face showed her contempt for the young girl at who she was now staring.

"The witness said the defendant was the shooter, no question about it," the older woman was not about to retract her statement.

The judge looked at me. "Counsel, you heard what the interpreter said, and that settles that, let's move on. Bailiff, bring in the jury, and young lady another outburst and you are in contempt of court, understand?" Angelica looked at me for guidance, and I shook my head in agreement and she said, "Yes, Sir."

I now had a plan to deal with this situation and returned to the counsel table without comment. Angelica was immediately writing me a note on my legal pad, "Are you going to let them get away with this?"

"No - just be patient and stay quiet," was my short written reply.

The state passed the witness.

Through the interpreter I asked; "José do you know this man seated next to me – the defendant?" I pointed.

"No, never seen him before that night and never seen him since."

"How often did you take your sons to visit and drink with their friends under that bridge?"

"Almost every weekend during the summer, while the weather is good."

"Do you drink, José?"

"Oh no, I am the driver, so I don't drink – just talk and eat tamales," José grinned and looked at the jury for their reaction. They were stone faced and humorless.

"Did you ever hear the dead man brag about the money he carried?" I asked - the jury leaned forward.

"Sí, I mean yea, he was a big mouth, always pointing at his shoes and telling everyone he kept all his money in his socks. I warned him to keep his business to himself but – he always drunk and talk *too much*."

"You only heard one shot that night is that right, you're sure about that?" I asked pointing my finger at the witness.

"Yea señor, only one shot.

"Did you see anyone else with a gun that night?"

"No, señor, only the pistolí that Jesús was holding; that only gun I saw."

"How did you know his name was Jesús?" I asked and stood up to show my concern.

José looked over at the interpreter for help – the jury followed his gaze and looked at the D.A. who continued to shuffle his notes and avoided looking at José's stare.

"I don't remember who told me his name," José finally replied.

"José, the truth is - you have a drinking problem yourself, don't you?"

"Objection," the D.A. was on his feet – "Badgering the witness again."

"Let's move on Mr. Wilson, is there some relevance to this case in your questions to this witness," the judge asked impatiently.

"Yes, your honor, I submit José was totally intoxicated that night and could not have remembered anything that happened and his testimony is useless and probably false."

"So what's your question, let's move on." The judge's impatience was growing.

"José, you were drinking that night, weren't you," I demanded.

"I might have drunk a couple of beers but I don't have a drinking problem," he was now defensive and nervous.

I picked up a file and handed it to José. "José, you have pled guilty to *two driving while intoxicated* cases in the last five years, haven't you?"

"Objection – your honor, please excuse the jury so we can argue this point," the frustrated prosecutor requested.

The jury was excused and after much argument – the judge ruled the two DWI convictions were not relevant to this case and ordered no further discussion concerning the matter. The judge was doing, as most criminal judges do, what he could to assist a prosecutor whose case was falling apart – not an unusual occurrence in American courtrooms. I had no more cross-examination for José.

The state rested their case. They had proven the deceased had died of a gunshot wound to the head. The state's entire case against Jesús now rested on their one eyewitness, José. No physical evidence was introduced to tie Jesús to the shooting. I needed to decide whether to call Jesús as a witness. His English was poor and the same woman court translator was going to be required to translate his testimony for the jury. The thought sent shivers up my back. Chaos would certainly occur when Jesús' family disagreed with any statement coming from the lips of the translator.

I have always been a firm believer that a defendant needs to testify in his own defense, but Jesús had one criminal conviction on his record; felony assault with a *firearm* that occurred years ago when he admitted he shot a man who had insulted and assaulted his wife at a drunken dance party. I really did not want the jury to hear about that event, and it was sure to be used against Jesús if he took the stand.

Instead of calling Jesús – I called Angelica to the stand, she could testify her father was home with the entire family the night the shooting took place and she did so. Most juries put little faith in close relatives testimony, but I did hit pay dirt when I asked the teenager if she could read and speak Spanish and English with equal ability.

"Angelica, are you enrolled in college now as a freshman?" I asked.

"Yes, and I work to help my family pay all our legal bills!" That drew smiles of respect from the jury.

"Did you hear José testify earlier today in this courtroom about seeing your father the night of the shooting?"

"Yes, sir."

"What did you hear José say about your father?"

"That my father looks like the shooter, he did not say father was the shooter."

"Objection, this girl is not a court-approved interpreter", the prosecutor was on his feet.

"Sustained, Counsel you know better that pull such a stunt in my courtroom, the jury will disregard that girl's last statement."

"Yes, your honor", I said and returned the smiles of the jury, the damage was done.

I passed the witness. The prosecutor wisely announced "No questions."

My investigator had warned me the medical examiner had refused to bring his portable x-ray viewer to court even though we had requested him to do so. That created a real dilemma for me. How do you show x-rays to a jury when you have no x-ray viewer? I looked at the outside window that was very near the jury box. In thirty minutes the afternoon sun would be streaming through that window. I needed to stall for time.

I called the M.E. to the stand and spent the next twenty minutes walking him through his many years of medical training and his participating in thousands of autopsies and the mechanics of an autopsy. Finally the judge had heard enough.

"Mr. Prosecutor, will you please stipulate the good doctor is very qualified so we can move on, Mr. Wilson is putting us all to sleep."

"So stipulated," the smiling D.A. announced.

"Doctor, I subpoenaed you and your reports and the deceased's x-rays to this trial, did I not?" I asked.

"That's correct," he replied, showing his contempt for me by rolling his eyes for the jury to see.

"You are paid by the county for your services, isn't that correct?" I asked.

"I am paid by Dallas County and they are reimbursed by Hill County for my services."

"Please have the court reporter mark as exhibits your x-rays of the body of the deceased in this matter." He handed the x-rays to the court reporter.

"Objection," the D.A. was on his feet, his voice tone showing his disdain for my offer of evidence. "The deceased has already been proven to have died from a gunshot to the head, so why do we need to expose the jury to the dead man's x-rays?"

Now it was my turn, I was on my feet – pointing at the D.A. "Their witnesses said they saw the deceased grab his stomach when he was supposedly shot in the head by my client. The state's own evidence proves the deceased died from a headshot. I want to see if the deceased was also shot in the stomach or elsewhere in his body that night."

The jury now exchanged glances and nodded their heads as they remembered the earlier conflicting proof introduced. The judge saw his dilemma and looked at me. "Mr. Wilson, this court and you don't have an x-ray viewer so you can't introduce x-rays into evidence when the witness cannot even view them for authentication purposes. You know better than that!"

The judge was moving in the direction of an excuse to deny the admission of the x-rays. He smelled a big problem coming for the state's case. I walked over and took the x-rays from the court reporter and selected the full body x-ray and held it up against the glass window near the jury box where the bright outside sunlight outlined the deceased's body so clearly that a gasp was heard from the jury.

The x-ray clearly showed three metal bullets in the deceased's body – one in the head, one in the chest, and one in the lower stomach. All three bullets were different in shape and size, but all were surprisingly clearly seen in the x-ray.

The courtroom was buzzing in anticipation of the next exchange.

"Doctor, in your professional opinion, are all three of those bullets in the dead man's body of different calibers, and if so what are those calibers?" I asked.

"Yes, they are all different calibers. The one in the skull is a .32 automatic, the chest bullet is a .38 revolver bullet and the one in the stomach is a .22 caliber bullet."

"Doctor, in your professional opinion which bullet caused the death of the deceased?"

"Each bullet was in a vital area. Any one of them could have caused the decedent's death."

"Doctor, can you tell by the entry width of the wound in the stomach of the .22 caliber bullet whether it was shot from a pistol or a rifle?"

"Yes, we can tell by the width of the entry wound whether the bullet was fired from a rifle or pistol."

"In your professional opinion was the .22 entry wound caused by a pistol?"

"No, it was a high velocity entry wound, so it was caused by a .22 caliber rifle, not a pistol."

"Doctor, in your professional opinion, which bullet struck the deceased first?"

"I have no opinion on that – I would have to witness the shootings in order to give such an opinion."

The doctor then testified he had mailed a full copy of his findings to the D.A.'s office several months earlier, along with the three actually removed bullets. The judge admitted the x-rays and M.E. reports into evidence. The looks on the jury faces convinced me to rest my case at that point and put the prosecutor immediately on the spot to explain about those three missing bullets. He also rested the state's case with no more witnesses or comments.

I made a motion for the court to enter a directed verdict of acquittal, which the evidence now supported and common justice demanded. The judge denied my motion, "The jury needs to decide this case and closing arguments are set for tomorrow morning," was his curt response.

The jurors looked at me as they filed out of their jury box, their expressions spoke louder than words: *"Thank God you showed us those x-rays before we convicted an innocent man."*

The next morning, after closing arguments and a short deliberation the jury returned with their verdict. They acquitted Jesús, who was reunited with his tearful family. Neither the D.A. nor the judge said anything to my client or me as they walked out of the courtroom with grim looks on their faces. We would meet again in the future.

Angelica called my office several days later, before she was to begin her employment. She was sick with a severe bout of morning sickness and afraid she wasn't going to be able to work for me after all – due to her "condition."

Such is life.

*A jury consists of twelve persons chosen to decide
who has the better lawyer.*
Robert Frost

6

A TRAGIC MOTOR VEHICLE COLLISION OCCURRED ON a state highway near my office one morning. I knew the family whose only son was scarred for life when his compact pickup collided with a large delivery truck while he was traveling to the local community college for his first day of class as a freshman. Sonny was a star athlete at the local high school.

His mangled vehicle and body had been plastered on the rear bumper of the parked eighteen-wheeler like a smashed bug. No one saw the collision or knew how it occurred. The truck driver was not at the scene. His story was that his truck had broken down and he walked away seeking assistance from his employer.

Nineteen-year old Sonny was on life support for several weeks, not expected to recover. The entire right side of his body had been smashed by the impact, from head to foot, fracturing most of his breakable bones.

Six months later, Sonny's parents appeared at my office requesting I represent them and their now disabled son in their claims against the local Coca-Cola franchise. I was surprised they had not retained a more experienced personal injury firm, but that mystery was quickly solved when they related that, "No one would take their case."

"There are no witnesses that saw the wreck and my son has complete amnesia of the events due to his trauma and injuries," the father said with downcast eyes, a look of defeat in his eyes. His wife joined in his look of hopelessness.

"The trucking company has offered us nothing, said our son was at fault. We are at our wits end."

I was a little annoyed that they only appeared in my office asking for assistance after being rejected by the larger plaintiffs' firms. I could clearly see the difficulties of proving a negligence case against such a well-financed defendant when you had no proof of negligence.

"We have to prove at least one act of negligence against the trucking company in order to prevail on this case, and the burden of proof is on us. So, what do you folks think caused the collision?" I asked. They shrugged and looked clueless.

"Sonny's life is ruined and it's all their fault! They need to compensate him and us for all the medical bills and his permanent disabilities!" The mother fairly screamed and her face immediately teared-up as her husband placed his arm around her shoulders.

"The physical evidence at the scene of the collision was no help," said the father. "The impact was so great and neither vehicle's exact location prior to the impact could be determined. The only clear facts are that Sonny drove into the rear of the parked truck, which had broken down on the side of the highway. Sonny has recovered enough to testify, but he has no memory of the wreck." The parents' eyes were begging for a miracle and a miracle worker – and I was the chosen one.

Sonny's damages were substantial, weeks in intensive care, months of rehabilitation, huge medical bills for doctors' care, hospitals and many follow-up surgeries. And, he was permanently disabled to some extent. The damages were certainly there, but without proof of liability, they meant nothing. My mind was racing. I understood how traumatic amnesia could block out memories. I'd been there myself. I suddenly felt a strange kinship with Sonny and his family. I needed time to digest and think about the facts of this case. I also wondered if Sonny really wanted to remember what happened to his body that fateful day. The human mind does not want to recall physical pain or mental anguish.

The parents had copies of all the police and investigation reports of the incident. I asked them to leave everything and let me review the matter with an accident reconstruction expert. "I will let you folks know if we have a reasonable chance of success."

"Oh, please, Bob!" the mother grabbed my arm and looked into my eyes, "Help Sonny and us on this case, you are our last hope!" The father reached for my hand in agreement. I smiled and walked them to our front office door, all the time wondering if I was just wasting my time and their hopes.

A review of the police reports and facts revealed Sonny had driven his small pickup at high speed into the rear of the parked delivery truck. The police interviews with the truck driver revealed that the truck blew a tire. The driver had parked the truck on the shoulder of the highway and placed warning cones at the truck's rear as required by law, then walked a mile to his nearby truck terminal for assistance.

Several items caught my eye – the investigation reports made no mention of finding any warning devices at the scene, or why the driver had not called in to his dispatcher and remained at the scene to warn oncoming traffic. The police investigator could make no determination of exact location of the delivery truck when impacted by Sonny's truck. The right front of Sonny's compact pickup was smashed totally, with its right front bumper and the motor block pushed back into Sonny's lap. Sonny must have turned his body to his left just at the point of impact, resulting in all his injuries being on the right side of his head and body.

The collision took place on a sharp right hand curve in the highway. It was a bright, sunny day, with no other traffic, so I suspected that Sonny would have avoided the truck if it was actually parked off the roadway as reported by the driver. But, Sonny would have had only a split second to avoid the truck if it was actually parked in his traffic lane. The actual location of that large truck and the existence of those warning cones in place at the time of impact became the crucial keys to winning or losing this case.

I called the lawyer representing the trucking company and asked if his client was willing to make a settlement offer. He laughed, and said, "Your clients are lucky they didn't get sued; Sonny caused this wreck and his case is worthless."

I wondered why the trucking company or their insurance company had not sued or filed a claim against my client if in fact he failed to keep a proper lookout and their truck was safely off the road with warning devices posted. Something did not seem right about this case. I decided to take it on – it was a long shot at best.

Sonny's parents promised to help pay for some of the litigation expenses we were about to incur, and they would be considerable, since we would need to retain unimpeachable experts to testify.

I prepared and filed their lawsuit for negligence at the Johnson County courthouse in Cleburne, Texas and the next year or so became what is known in legal jargon as the *discovery period,* when under state court rules of procedure, both parties, plaintiff and defendant, discover all the evidence that the other party intends to use at trial. No surprises are allowed in courts anymore, no ambushes.

Many hours and much money were used to depose the medical providers in order to prove the extent and duration of Sonny's injuries and his past and future medical expenses. An accountant would testify to Sonny's past and future lost earnings.

I took the delivery truck driver's deposition and was convinced he was not being truthful. His story about needing to walk to obtain assistance just did not pass the smell test. There were closer telephones and he was in constant contact with his dispatcher. His version of where he placed his warning cones was suspect and he was vague about exactly where he had a blowout and exactly where he parked his truck before walking away. When I asked him why he did not use a closer phone to call for assistance, he gave no reason, avoiding eye contact with me. He also admitted his truck was still drivable, but he pulled over and stopped when he heard a tire blowout. He agreed he was about a mile from the truck terminal and could have probably driven his truck there, but he wanted permission first from his supervisors before he moved his truck. He was hiding something – I just did not know what.

Sonny's deposition was taken and he was able to clearly describe his injuries, current limitations, and his dashed dreams of playing college sports. Of course, when asked about the actual day of the wreck, he testified it was just a "complete blank," he did not even remember driving that morning. The defense lawyer smiled at me – knowing our proof was very weak, the favored position for insurance lawyers in serious injury cases.

I needed to crank up my powers of imagination and come up with a miracle or we had just wasted a great amount of time and money. I desperately needed proof the delivery truck was unlawfully parked with no warning devices and a hazard to approaching traffic on the day of the collision.

One morning I drove to the collision location arriving several minutes before the time of day of Sonny's collision. A bread truck stopped at a nearby store and proceeded to unload a rack of bread. I drove over and talked to the driver.

"Did you happen to hear or see the collision between the pickup and 18 wheeler delivery truck across the street about a year ago?"

"I heard about it, but I was in the store when it happened and did not know something happened until the sirens arrived," he said.

"Did you see the driver of the truck anywhere?" I asked.

"Yes, I saw him running out of the same store I was in when he heard the sirens arriving, hollering – 'That's my truck!'"

"Did you see any warning devices set up around that Coke truck?"

"No, but I drove up from the opposite direction, so I could have missed them," he said.

I got his name and address and thanked him. I now had proof the truck driver had lied under oath about his whereabouts before the collision that day.

It occurred to me that crime victims are sometimes hypnotized to remember traumatic events and their attacker's description. Why not try this with Sonny? I would need a medical doctor as an expert. I researched respected medical doctors in the area to see if any of them was a recognized specialist in treating patients through hypnosis.

I found a doctor in Dallas who specialized in treating terminal cancer patients who were suffering and in great anguish and distress. He was known as a miracle worker with his ability to reduce their suffering from cancer treatments though hypnotism. I discussed with Sonny and his parents the idea of hypnotizing Sonny for the purpose of trying to medically treat him for his post-traumatic depression and to see if he could recall the details of the collision. They were agreeable and grateful for help with their son's increasing depression.

I talked with the good doctor and he was keenly interested in trying his techniques on Sonny. We both agreed the session needed to be fully videotaped and audibly recorded for the purpose of introducing it into evidence at the trial as medical treatment evidence of Sonny's trauma caused depression. Hopefully, under hypnosis, Sonny would remember the facts of the wreck. The doctor's interview and treatment session would be part of *Sonny's medical treatment,* and therefore admissible evidence at the trial.

I prepared a list of questions I wanted the doctor to ask Sonny under hypnosis about the events before and during the collision. The doctor called me following his session with Sonny and excitedly said, "He remembered everything that happened. He answered all your questions fully." The doctor's office mailed me a copy of the videotape – it was everything I needed to prove our case – a miracle had occurred after all.

A month later the case was called to trial and a jury was seated. The burden of proof was on me and when I gave my opening statement to the jury, the defense counsel suddenly stiffened when I calmly stated, "We will prove the large truck was unlawfully parked, partially blocking the main highway, with no warning devices deployed to warn approaching vehicles, such as Sonny. The truck driver abandoned the truck and walked next door to take a break."

I called the bread truck driver first to testify he saw the driver of the Coca – Cola truck in nearby store and saw him run to the scene when he heard the approaching sirens. The two defense counsels exchanged worried glances.

I called the doctor to the stand next and had him recite his impressive medical background and expertise in hypnosis treatments of patients.

"Doctor, as part of Sonny's medical treatment to relieve depression and anxiety, did you have him submit to a session of hypnosis?"

"Yes sir, in my medical office I placed him under hypnosis in isolation from any other persons or distractions and took him back to the morning of his injuries."

"Did you make a video tape of the session and is it your routine to always video tape those sessions?"

"Yes, I always video the sessions and later allow the patient to watch the video in order that the patient's mind can try to understand and deal with suppressed feelings of pain and anxiety."

"Doctor, we have set up a video player and monitor for you to show the jury that video of your treatment session." Objections were made and overruled.

The jury and judge suddenly came to attention as the video monitor showed Sonny reclining with his eyes closed on a couch in the doctor's office. The doctor's voice could clearly be heard on the video, "Sonny – I want you to think back in time to the day you were injured in your truck on your way to college that morning. What time did you leave your house that morning?"

Sonny's dream like voice answered clearly – "About seven thirty in the morning, I was leaving for my first day of class at the college, I was driving my Ranger pickup."

"What highway did you take that morning?"

"Highway 174 heading south toward Cleburne."

"How fast were you driving that morning?"

"Fifty-five, the speed limit," he replied.

"As you approached Cleburne did you encounter a sharp curve in the highway?"

"Yes, and suddenly I saw a huge trailer truck was stopped dead in the road ahead of me; I slammed on my breaks and turned the steering wheel, but it was too late and I turned away from the impact."

"Did you see any warning devices or flashing lights as you approached the truck?"

"No, there was no warning at all – nothing – it was just suddenly there in my face."

"Do you remember the impact?"

"Yes," at this point Sonny's voice took on an unnatural high pitch that sent a chill through every person in that courtroom.

"My right foot and leg are being crushed – I feel the bones breaking," Sonny suddenly screamed loudly and everyone jumped.

"Oh God, please God," Sonny is screaming loudly now – "My arm and shoulder bones are breaking" – his blood curdling screams vibrated in the courtroom – several women jurors are now holding their shaking hands to their faces, staring at the monitor with fear in their eyes.

"Please God!" he is screaming even louder now – "Please help me, my skull is cracking, my ear is being torn away."

Sonny suddenly became very quiet and sighs could be heard from the jurors. Without warning – Sonny's body suddenly jerks violently on the couch and another gut wrenching scream comes from his lips – "Mommy, please mommy – help me! Help me!" He collapsed back on the couch – his ordeal over.

The women jurors were now openly sobbing or covering their faces. The men on the jury are looking down at the floor, trying to show no emotion, but several had hands to their brows to conceal their feelings.

The judge suddenly stood and cleared his throat. "Let's take a thirty minute break," and without another word, turned around and walked out of his rear door, leaving the jurors to care for themselves. The jurors stumbled out of their seats and quickly retired to the waiting jury room behind their seats.

The defense lawyers looked over at me like two deer caught in on-coming headlights. "Let's talk Bob, in the hallway, outside." My clients looked at me for direction. "Wait here please - be right back," I was gone before they could reply.

The lead defense lawyer turned to me in the hallway and in a low voice asked, "How much will it take to settle this mess?"

It took a lot.

After the court recess was over – all parties and counsel announced to the court a settlement had been reached and the judge thanked everyone for their time and cooperation and released the jury and adjourned court. My clients were very happy and kept shaking my hand and hugging me for helping justice to prevail and the truth to come forward.

They soon departed and when I walked to my car I noticed one of the male jurors standing near my vehicle – waiting for me. I offered my hand and thanked him for his service. I recognized him to be a high school coach from a nearby town.

He had a strange look on his face and said, "That was quite a show in there you put on – good thing for your client you settled the case – you know why?"

I felt a chill run down my spine – this was not going to be good – I could tell by his demeanor.

"Because, I was going to vote against your client – he was just speeding and not watching the road that day – like most teenagers."

I did not reply and shrugged my shoulders and drove away without a word – making a mental note never to let a high school coach ever sit on any jury of mine – I didn't need the grief of trying to convince a fool the earth was round.

And God said: "Let there be Satan, so people don't blame everything on me. And let there be lawyers, so people don't blame everything on Satan'.
George Burns

7

ONE OF MY DEER HUNTING BUDDIES CALLED and asked me to "do him a favor" and talk to his grown daughter, Betsy, about her husband's *situation*. I told him, without asking for more information, "Sure, what are friends for, tell her to call and make an appointment." Next time - I will make further inquiry.

In short order, Betsy came to my office to hire me to defend her husband on a burglary charge in Huntsville, Texas; hometown of the Texas Prison System. A worse place to defend a criminal defendant cannot be imagined. At least one-half of any jury panel will be composed of current or retired law enforcement employees; mostly prison guards.

I informed Betsy of my own personal distaste for thieves and burglars. My house had recently been burglarized and my valuable firearm collection stolen, never to be seen again.

She was certain her husband was innocent and being framed by an old girlfriend in Georgia. I found that a little suspicious, but agreed to go to the local county jail where her husband, Kenneth Evans was being held, awaiting transfer to Huntsville for trial. His two co-defendants were already in Huntsville.

I met the defendant, Kenneth the next day in the lawyer interview room – my first impression of him was that he was a professional burglar. He had the look, the personality and prison background that made him an excellent candidate for a mandatory life sentence as a three-time loser or as they say in the business, *The Bitch*. Kenneth already had two prior burglary convictions. One more and he was history. His wife and young son would then be on their own, for good. His wife was a sweetheart, petite, pretty and a woman that loved outlaws. There are many women of that cut in Texas; all you have to do is go watch on visitor's day at the state prisons. It never ceased to amaze me.

As he talked, though, Kenneth made a convincing case for himself, telling a story of a woman scorned in Georgia that sounded plausible. He was unclear as to why he had been in Georgia in the first place – but he was not on trial for being an unfaithful husband. I agreed to defend him.

When I notified the D.A. in Huntsville of my representation, he supplied me with a copy of the indictment that named three defendants in what turned out to be the one of the largest burglaries in the history of Huntsville – at the largest jewelry story. The other two defendants had been sitting in that local county jail for many months, their court-appointed attorneys stood ready to perform their part at eating at the county's legal feeding trough. The defendants had yet to meet their legal counsels. The D.A. was anxious to put all three of these characters on a show trial as an example of what happens to strangers who decide to rob local citizens or their businesses.

A week before the Huntsville case was to go to trial I was knee deep in a bitter three way custody trial concerning a baby boy. Mother vs. her mother vs. the child's father – it does not get any worse than that. I informed the Huntsville judge and D.A. in advance that I was already set for trial on an older child custody trial in Fort Worth and could not appear at their current trial date. They were unmoved and unconcerned with my dilemma.

The trial evidence in the Fort Worth case finally ended and the custody determination went to the jury after five days of testimony and rancor. The lawyers involved were all sitting in the judge's chambers waiting for the jury to return a verdict when the judge's phone rang, he answered the phone and put it on speaker phone "Yes," the judge began, "What can I do for you?"

"Where is lawyer Wilson?" – an angry voice was heard on the other end, "He was supposed to be here in Huntsville District Court picking a jury at nine o'clock this morning! This is District Judge Brownly."

The judge's chamber became very quiet and the blood drained from my head.

"Wilson is sitting right here in my office – we are waiting for a jury verdict on a case that lasted five days." The worried judge was looking at me for guidance.

"Put him on the phone," the voice sounding angrier and louder.

"Yes, Judge," I said politely.

"Get your ass down here now or you will be held in contempt of court," the distant voice was almost screaming.

I gathered my thoughts, and firmly answered his challenge: "Judge I filed a motion for continuance in your court and you and the D.A. know I am in trial in Fort Worth. I can't be in two towns at the same time and this is an older case," I plead my case.

"You'll be here at one o'clock today or I will issue an arrest warrant for you." *Click*, the conversation was over.

"What do I do Judge?" I asked the embarrassed nearby judge.

"I will release you to go to Huntsville, and call you on the phone when and if this jury returns with a verdict. Find a local lawyer to cover for you here tomorrow in case the jury adjourns for the night."

"Okay Judge, I'm gone."

I explained my situation to my horrified client, the child's mother, and drove to my office to pick up the other file and hit the road for the impossible appearance time of one o'clock p.m. on a trip that was sure to take over three hours at unsafe speeds. It was already eleven o'clock in the morning.

I drove like a demon to Huntsville, arriving at two thirty - one and one half hours late. I sprang up the stone stairs into the packed district courtroom to be greeted by one hundred potential jurors who stared at me like I was the devil incarnate as I walked up to the bench that housed the impatient sitting judge and introduced myself in front of the packed courtroom.

He refused to shake my hand and in front of the three defendants, their two appointed counsel; all the potential jurors and a packed courtroom of spectators he started his diatribe, "Mr. Wilson, all these people have been sitting here since nine o'clock this morning waiting for you. Have you no respect for this court, or this county's residents, or even your own client?" – he said as he looked down at me from his high bench like I was road kill, and he was driving a Mack.

I turned away from the judge and looked at Kenneth, my client, sitting by himself at the counsel table, his hair in a tangled mess, his unshaven face; his soiled and wrinkled clothes clearly marking him as the bum that happened to be on trial for his life. Kenneth looked like a whipped dog. Each trial lawyer must decide early in his career if he is going to be a judge's doormat or as they say in the trade – a *renegade barrister*. I chose to be the latter.

I calmly walked over to the nervous court reporter – "Ms. Reporter, be sure you take down everything I am about to say - verbatim." Her wide-eyed face nodded rapidly as she glanced at the judge. I walked back to stand directly under the judge's bench and turned on my heels to face the packed large courtroom of well over a hundred icy stares.

"Folks," my booming voice could be clearly heard not only in the courtroom, but also on the entire floor of the courthouse. "I am Bob Wilson, attorney for defendant Kenneth Evans. I have been in trial in Fort Worth, Texas district court since last week – that jury is currently in deliberations – I was ordered by this judge to leave my client there without counsel and be in this court at one o'clock today or go to jail."

It was now completely silent in the courtroom. I had everyone's attention. "This judge and this D.A. have known for two weeks that I could not be here today, but they announced to you I had not yet appeared this morning and had you folks sit in this courtroom for five hours getting madder and madder at me when they both knew full well I was in another town unable to be here."

The judge cleared his throat; I ignored him and walked over and faced my client. "If you will look at my client – you will notice his hair is dirty and uncombed, he hasn't been allowed to shave in days, his clothes are soiled and wrinkled and he looks like the bum they want you to think he is." Kenneth's face was turning bright red as I continued, "There is no way my client can get a fair trial when you folks, the jury panel, have already been poisoned by this court and D.A.'s actions today – I therefore have no choice but to make a motion that this jury panel be stricken in its entirety and this judge remove himself as the trial judge – because he is so openly prejudicial against me and my client he has denied my client due process of law and has created a mockery here today of the American criminal justice system right in front of your eyes."

The prospective jurors were exchanging anxious glances and several were now smiling at me with looks of admiration, but most of them just sat motionless, some with dropped jaws and raised eyebrows – some looking only at the floor.

I turned and addressed the court, "I need the court to rule on my motion to strike this entire jury panel, declare a mistrial, and disqualify yourself as the presiding judge." The judge was white as a sheet and his quivering voice could be barely heard.

"Court adjourned for thirty minutes – please clear the courtroom, Mr. Bailiff, except for legal counsel and their clients." The courtroom cleared quickly and noisily. The judge's wrinkled face finally spoke.

"Mr. Wilson – seems we started off on the wrong foot, I will instruct the jury panel that it is not your fault for the delays this morning; I will instruct the sheriff to return your client to the jail and see that he has a haircut, clean clothes and a shower," he looked around the courtroom and continued, "Do I have your permission to excuse this jury panel until nine o'clock tomorrow morning and move forward with jury selection at that time – and will you withdraw all your stated motions?"

"Yes, sir," I replied. "When I hear the court instruct the jurors that I have no responsibility for the delays and confusion today and that the sheriff has been ordered to provide decent facilities for my client – then I will be glad to withdraw my pending motions."

I was going to hold his feet to the fire, I had him by the balls and I was squeezing, slowly. He looked at me and I looked back at him for several minutes – two junkyard dogs smelling each other. It was going to be a tense trial. The young D.A. had yet to open his mouth. He stood and shook my hand, "Welcome to Huntsville, Mr. Wilson."

The judge turned to his clerk – "Tell the jury to please take their seats." He then proceeded to address the jury in a different tone – completely clearing me of any wrongdoing, apologizing for my client's appearance and asking forgiveness from the jury panel for the court's *misunderstandings*. He then adjourned court until nine o'clock the next morning. Several of the courtroom spectators could be heard whispering – "Who's this guy think he is – God?"

I keenly watched each potential juror's reaction to the judge's announcement. Some smiled at me and nodded – some frowned and looked away. Jury selection had already begun – they just did not realize it.

If a town could be labeled *a prison town* - Huntsville, Texas would be its poster child. The largest building in town was the original high walled state prison with its imposing guard towers looking down on the town itself. The outskirts of town were endless rows of prison buildings and their heavily fenced and guarded prison premises. The economy of the town was the huge prison complexes and to a lesser extent, the small liberal arts college nearby.

The most modern motel in town was the Holiday Inn. I checked in for the entire week. I asked the talkative desk clerk, "Who's driving the motor vehicles parked outside that have federal government and State of Georgia plates?"

My suspicions were quickly confirmed, "F.B.I. and Georgia cops – here for the big trial – are you involved?" – the clerk asked with excitement in his voice.

"Maybe," I smiled and left it at that, "Too early to tell for sure. I think I know those Feds – what rooms are they in?" I asked with interest.

"Room 8, two Agents in the same room. Guess they are too tight to rent two rooms."

After changing my sweat soaked clothes I drove over to the county jail to speak with my client. Kenneth smiled when he was brought into the lawyer conference room. "You always make such an entrance?" he asked.

"Only when I need to," I replied, "That ornery old judge doesn't like me much."

Kenneth leaned forward, as to share a big secret, "The boys want you to represent them too – they do not trust their court-appointed lawyers."

I was too surprised to speak by his comment – I just looked at him.

"Their asshole lawyers want them to plead out for five years each and testify against me – they refused the shitty deal."

"Well, we sure don't want them to do that do we? I will ask the judge if he will appoint me on both their cases. None of you guys can testify anyway because all three of you have burglary convictions. If the jury learns about those priors, they will convict you guys – regardless of the evidence."

I discussed some minor details of the case with him and asked him "Where is your wife and son, and your family? They need to be here to support you."

"Back in Fort Worth, she won't come – doesn't want Steven to see me in jail or chains," he said lowering his gaze.

I stood up, "She must come – and bring the boy and your parents – if the jury doesn't think your family cares about you – why should they? Tell them to sit in the courtroom behind you and you smile at them every now and then – let the jury see you have a family that cares about you."

The facts of this case were rather unusual. The police had no direct evidence against the three defendants. My discovery motions had yielded the following evidence that the D.A. intended to use to obtain convictions: All three defendants were Georgia boys – supposedly members of the "Georgia Mafia" – whatever that was. All three defendants were related family members – cousins or something. They had lived together off and on in Georgia and Texas, depending on opportunities to make money.

On one of their many trips to Georgia, Kenneth had met a lively young lady at a strip club and they became *more than friends*. Kenneth finally told her he was married and he and the boys moved back to Texas. She had a wicked jealous streak and told him, "You'll be sorry." She wasn't kidding. She went to the Georgia Bureau of Investigation – G.B.I. – and reported to them that Kenneth and the other two fellows were safecrackers from Texas and had admitted to her they burglarized a jewelry store in Huntsville, Texas a year earlier.

Other than the testimony of the former stripper, "the Georgia Peach" – the only other evidence against the three defendants were two local men who supposedly picked all three defendants out of a police photo lineup. The two witnesses just happened to notice and remember the three defendants starring into the closed jewelry store on the Saturday night prior to the break-in.

The police investigation reports revealed that several men had cut a hole in the roof of one business and then cut another hole in the connecting wall into the jewelry store next door. They then proceeded to drill and cut their way into the large steel and concrete safe which contained the jewelry store's valuables. The burglars would have needed at least twelve hours to complete their little caper and get away clean with the jewelry. No one heard or saw anything of suspicion during the burglary.

I immediately suspected the two so-called eyeball witnesses were either mistaken in their identification or just plain publicity hounds. None of the stolen jewelry was traced to my clients; none of it ever recovered. All three defendants were broke and Kenneth's parents and wife were paying me, so I wondered how safecrackers with such talent could become so broke, so fast, unless my clients were completely innocent, as they loudly proclaimed.

I spent most of the night reviewing the statements of the state's three witnesses looking for inconsistencies. I had a hunch what the D.A. would do before trial the next morning and I was correct.

The trial was to officially start at nine o'clock in the morning but I quietly walked into the courthouse much earlier, while it was very quiet and mostly empty. I walked up to the floor above where the trial courtroom was and positioned myself where I could see the double doors entrance into the lower floor courtroom by looking down from above through the open circular dome, which rose from the basement floor to the ceiling of the courthouse.

I was soon rewarded for my efforts. Two deputies brought the three defendants, now clean–shaven and neatly dressed, into the lower courtroom, and seated them at the defense table – which is always, of course, positioned on the far side from where the jury seats. The D.A. always had the counsel table near the jury – an event that never ceased to anger me as a defense attorney. One day, an appeals court with some backbone will put a stop to that universal and unfair practice in American courtrooms.

The deputies removed the defendants' handcuffs and took their seats at the back of the courtroom, guarding the entrance door. Sure enough, within a few minutes I heard voices and noise on the steps leading to the courtroom. I watched as the D.A. and two unknown men walked up to the courtroom entrance doors and looked into the courtroom through the courtroom glass doors.

"That's them;" – the D.A. said and pointed his finger toward the seated defendants. His two male companions placed their faces to the glass door and stared for several minutes at the seated defendants. "Can you remember where they are sitting?" the D.A. asked. "Just point them out when the time comes." The two men nodded and the three of them walked back down the steps and disappeared into the D.A.'s office.

"Two down, one to go," I said out loud to myself and walked down to the courtroom floor and sat with my clients until court officially began.

The judge was in a completely different mood when the proceedings began and without argument, granted the two other co-defendants' requests to excuse their court-appointed attorneys and appointed me to represent all defendants for the duration.

The jury panel was composed mostly of state workers, either from the prison system or the local college campus. Many jurors wanted to explain privately why they could not be fair and impartial jurors. They had been burglary victims themselves – they were excused.

A jury was finally selected by the end of the day, with only two state prison employees. It could have been worse, at least there were two college professors seated.

I noticed an attractive young woman now sitting in the witness room at lunchtime. She was brightly dressed, someone who enjoyed attention. I pointed her out to my clients and they confirmed my suspicions – "That is the Georgia Peach alright, dressed to kill, like a coral snake," they said almost in unison.

It was about four thirty when the jury was seated and sworn. The judge adjourned court for the day. "We will start with the testimony when everyone is refreshed in the morning."

I exited the courtroom quickly and made a beeline to the Holiday Inn and watched from my room to see if "Ms. Peach" appeared and who was providing her transportation and room and board. She soon arrived in a white Ford sedan with government plates. Two suited gentlemen assisted her out and the three entered Room 8 and stayed therein. At eight o'clock I assumed they were in for the night and gave up my observation post and went to eat dinner and plan strategy.

The next morning I was dressed and watching Room 8 by six o'clock. Sure enough at six thirty the two suited agents and "Ms. Peach" emerged and loaded up the government sedan and drove away. I was beginning to look forward to the approaching fireworks – win or lose – this was going to be an interesting case for all involved.

The state's evidence was enough for a conviction, but relied too heavily on eyewitnesses and was lacking physical evidence. That was about to change by an unforeseen event.

The courtroom was already full and waiting for the judge to appear and give his blessing to the proceedings. I noticed the female owner of the jewelry store was seated directly behind the prosecutor's table. She gave me a *go to hell look* and looked away like she had stepped in something stinky.

The courtroom doors in the back of the courtroom opened and Kenneth's wife and precious little boy walked in followed by Kenneth's long suffering parents. They looked at me for guidance and I motioned for them to sit behind the defendants and me.

Many local citizens had filled up the empty courtroom benches on both sides. The courtroom was full and an air of excitement filled the benches. The judge walked in and told the bailiff to "Bring in the jury," which always assembled in the jury room.

The twelve jurors were in the process of walking from the jury room to their seats in the courtroom when a woman's blood-curdling scream pierced the silence and everyone jumped, several bystanders stood and ran for the doors.

I whirled around to see the owner of the jewelry store standing and pointing her finger at Betsy, my client's wife, who looked innocently at me for help while her face turned bright red. The storeowner removed her hands from her mouth and yelled at the top of her voice, "That's one of my stolen rings on that woman's hand – that is one of my stolen rings! Arrest her!"

Two deputies walked quickly over to Betsy and grabbed her arms and pulled her up to a standing position. The courtroom erupted with noise, everyone talking and shouting at once. The twelve jurors froze in their tracks, unsure of what to do next.

The judge looked at me and he read my mind: he knew I was entitled to a mistrial immediately. He also knew that since a jury had been seated and sworn in, I had strong grounds to invoke a defense of double jeopardy to a second trial because the state's witness had caused this mistrial. The judge acted quickly and pointed at the bailiff, "Take the jury back to their room; jurors, do not in any manner discuss whatever you may have just heard or seen this morning – understand?"

The jurors all nodded their heads; several of them kept trying to get a better look at Betsy's hand so they could see what all the excitement was about.

I was mad and surprised at the same time. It was an obvious setup and my client's wife had walked right into the trap and was looking at me to save her from being jailed.

The judge had a grim face when he announced a thirty-minute recess and called the lawyers and his court reporter to his chambers. Before the judge could stand I spoke up. "Judge, I request my client's wife not be arrested until after we confer on this matter – she is not going anyplace."

The judge looked at Betsy and nodded – "Stay where you sit Ma'am until I tell you otherwise." Betsy was now white as a sheet and her five-year-old son was holding onto her and crying.

The two deputies let go of her and asked her to remove all her rings and place them in an evidence bag. She looked at me for guidance and I nodded for her to comply. I had to make many fundamental decisions quickly concerning this incident and they needed to be correct decisions.

When I walked into the Judge's chambers he was seated, with his booted feet on his desk. The D.A. had a silly grin on his face when he looked at me – like "Let's see how you get your clients out of this, Mr. Smart Ass."

"Mr. Wilson, let me hear what you have to say about that little commotion that just took place," the judge knew everyone involved was now skating on thin ice.

I took a deep breath, "Judge, I don't want my client's wife arrested. If the jury thinks she had stolen property in her possession, then this case must end in a mistrial immediately. If the state tries to retry these guys it will be after the appellate courts have decided whether double jeopardy has attached to these cases. It could be ten years before these issues are decided."

The D.A. was no longer smiling.

"Wilson's right, Mr. Prosecutor, this case is now in a big mess. Why did you let your witness pull such a stupid stunt?

"Judge, I am totally innocent, I had no idea Mrs. Clark was going to spot some of her jewelry in the courtroom," he lied.

I could hear in my mind the conservation he probably had with his witness, "Mrs. Clark, our evidence is weak. We have no physical connection between your stolen jewelry and these defendants. We need proof those ex-cons have possession of some of that stolen jewelry." She had done her best to solve the D.A.'s dilemma.

"Judge, I ask you to release my client's wife on her own recognizance with no bond. She is quite innocent. I request that you instruct the jury to disregard everything they saw and heard in the courtroom this morning and tell them it was nothing but a misunderstanding. Also, Mrs. Clark is forbidden to testify on the witness stand that she thinks my client's wife was wearing her stolen jewelry."

With that the D.A. jumped up – "Judge that is our best evidence. You can't exclude it, we need it." The D.A. was whining like a child's whose toy was taken.

"Otherwise, Judge," I interrupted, "I request a mistrial and bail bonds be set for all three defendants."

The judge looked sternly at the prosecutor, "If you have a weak case, what are we doing here in the first place?"

"We have a good case, just little physical evidence. Okay, Mrs. Clark will keep her mouth shut about the ring. We have federal and state agents here from Georgia and the county is paying for everything. We need to move forward and try this case only one time."

With that quick settlement, the jury returned to be told *to forget what they may have heard or seen in the courtroom –* fat chance of that. The jurors looked immediately to where my client's wife and boy sat. She smiled innocently as I had instructed her to do – "And keep your hands folded in your lap." The stage was now set and the actors ready to perform...

*A man who never graduated from school might steal
from a freight car. But a man who attends college and
graduates as a lawyer might steal the whole railroad.*
Theodore Roosevelt

8

THE STATE'S FIRST WITNESS WAS THE LOCAL *city walker.* Every town has one, a man or woman that walks the streets everyday – with no destination or purpose in mind. They smile and wave at anyone who looks their way and most people try to avoid a conversation.

The witness was neatly dressed, well groomed and was happy to be the center of attention, nodding and smiling at everyone but the defendants and me.

The prosecutor asked, "Jim, what did you see that Saturday afternoon that caught your attention outside the jewelry store?"

I could have objected at such an obvious leading question but I chose not to interrupt – I would soon have my way with Mr. Jim.

"I was walking by Mrs. Clark's jewelry store and saw three strangers starring into the closed store – they looked suspicious to me."

The prosecutor stood and walked over to the witness, "Jim do you see those three strangers, those men, anywhere in this courtroom?"

Jim immediately turned and extended his arm and finger pointing at my clients sitting red-faced next to me at the counsel table.

"That's them!" Jim was loud and animated as the jury's eyes focused on all four of us sitting uncomfortable at the counsel table, even I felt a little guilty.

The prosecutor walked over to the court reporter and proudly announced, "Let the record show that the witness has identified the three defendants as the three men he observed in front of the closed jewelry store shortly before the break in."

Another misstatement of facts, but I let it pass without objection. Let them dig their hole as deep as possible, I thought. The witness was passed for cross-examination. I stood and walked until I was standing near the edge of the jury box, which forced the witness to look at the jury and me at the same time.

"Jim, when is the last time you have seen these three defendants?"

"About one year ago, the day before the robbery," Jim's voice was losing its boldness and was now little more than a loud whisper; he was already on the defensive.

"Have their appearances changed much since you last saw them?"

"Why yes, all three men had full beards on the day I saw them."

"These fellows are all clean-shaven, right?" I asked, pointing at the group of three.

"Yes, but I remember their features because I suspected they were up to something – three men looking into a closed jewelry store is something that looks suspicious to me."

"Did you give a description of those men to the police department when you found out about the break-in?" I asked holding up a copy of the Jim's police report description given a year earlier.

"It says here you never really saw their faces because they all had full beards, all wore hats, and never looked at you. Did you tell the police that?"

"I don't remember exactly what I told the police," the witness was starting to shift his considerable weight in the wooden witness chair.

"Jim – can I call you Jim?" I asked. The witness nodded.

"Where were you going that day you say you saw these three fellows?"

"Nowhere, just walking around town."

"Where do you work?"

"I don't – I am on disability."

"What is your disability?"

"Sometimes I lose contact."

"Lose contact with what?"

"Everything."

"Do you take medication for this problem?"

"Yes, supposed to take it twice daily, but, sometimes I forget."

"Jim, this is serious business here today, not a game. These fellows are going to prison if this jury believes your story, you understand the seriousness?"

"Yes sir, absolutely."

"So why did you lie to the jury a few minutes ago when you testified under oath that you had not seen these men since the day before the break-in? You knew better, didn't you?"

Jim looked at the D.A. for help – the jurors saw the look of fear in his face – the D.A. looked down at his papers – Jim looked down at the floor.

"Jim, look at me – I want you to tell the jury the truth," my voice becoming louder and shriller. Tell the jury the D.A. brought you to this courtroom early this morning before anyone else was here and pointed out those three men to you and told you to remember where they were seated, didn't he?" Jim turned bright red.

The D.A. was on his feet objecting, "Objection – badgering the witness."

"Overruled. Mr. Wilson, where are you going with this line of questions? You cannot make the D.A. into a witness – I will not allow it, understand?"

"Your honor, I may have to put the D.A. on the stand if Jim does not tell the truth. I ask the court to question this witness if he refuses to answer my questions truthfully."

I continued, "Jim – one last time before I request the court question you. Didn't you and another man look through those glass doors to this courtroom this morning at seven thirty and were told by this D.A. that those three men sitting there are the defendants on trial – remember that conversation now?"

Jim wilted like a fly in the hot sun. "Yes, I told the D.A. I probably could not recognize the men if they no longer had beards."

A murmur arose from the courtroom and the jurors glanced at each other and then at the red-faced D.A. I was now ready with the kill shot – "So who was the other man with you this morning when the D.A. pointed out my clients to you?"

"Barney, the sneaker man. He saw those three bearded men that Saturday also looking into that jewelry store. He said he wasn't sure he could recognize them either without beards."

The several jurors looked at me and shook their heads ever so slightly. The state's two eyeball witnesses were not going to be of much value to the state now. The *Georgia Peach* was now their only hope for a conviction.

Barney testified next, he looked more like a circus clown than a businessman. He was a large man, over three hundred pounds, and at least six and a half feet tall. His colorful shirt was too small for him and his pants too large and baggy. He wore sneakers, private label tennis shoes.

He testified like he was scripted, repeating the same story as Jim. Barney's Sneaker Store was only two stores away from the scene of the break-in. Barney saw the three strangers, all bearded, walk by his store about closing time on that Saturday afternoon. He noticed them stop and peer into the closed jewelry store for several minutes. The men had their backs to him but he noticed that they all wore sneakers – he always looked at peoples' feet – a trait that was automatic to him.

Barney admitted on the stand, "I was afraid I could not recognize those men after so long a time so the D.A. volunteered to point them out to me – which he did this morning. They certainly look different without beards – but they are the right size and shape."

I had wondered why, when the G.B.I. arrested two of the Georgia boys they had seized all their shoes – the same thing happened when the F.B.I. arrested Kenneth Evans. They were looking for those sneakers, but no evidence of the defendants' shoes had been introduced as yet – I smelled a rat in the woodpile.

"Barney, how long have you been in the sneaker business?"

"All my life – it is my business and passion. I even collect old tennis shoes."

"Barney, did the police ever show you any shoe prints from the scene of the jewelry store break-in and ask your assistance?"

"Yes, they did – how did you know?" Barney seemed shaken by my questions.

"Describe the shoe prints the police asked you to examine."

"The police had photos of clear tennis shoe tracks found inside the store. The burglars had walked in a white powder that was all over the floor. After the burglars cut open the safe with cutting torches, the white powder used as fire proofing in the walls of the safe was scattered everywhere on the floor of that store."

"Did you give the police your opinion of the brand name and size of the tennis shoe prints found at the scene?" My heart was now pounding in anticipation.

"Yes, they were a rather unusual Nike shoe, size twelve."

"Barney, did you say size twelve?"

"Yea, in my opinion the Nike shoes worn by one of the bad guys, was size twelve."

The prosecutor was on his feet objecting. He knew where I was going and he saw a train wreck bearing down on him. "Judge, this witness cannot give his opinion about the shoe size by looking at a photograph," the prosecutor's voice cracked.

"Overruled, this is cross-examination."

"Barney, walk over and look at these three defendants' feet and tell me if any of them have size twelve feet?"

"Objection, the defense cannot expect this witness to make such a comparison."

"Sustained," the judge ruled with sharpness in his voice. He knew the state was in trouble. "Mr. Wilson, that question is not proper – move on."

I walked over to the three defendants and told them to remove their shoes and then walked over to the court reporter and had her mark those shoes as trial exhibits and handed the three pairs of shoes to Barney. "Are any of these three sets of shoes size twelve?"

Barney looked closely at the six shoes – "No, none of these are size twelve, largest is a size ten and a half – Double D."

I noticed that the two jurors who were college professors were now rolling their eyes and appeared to me to be losing confidence in the state's evidence.

The judge excused the jury until the next morning and requested everyone else remain so other important issues could be addressed. The D.A. announced that he wanted to file criminal charges against my client's wife for possession of stolen property and have the storeowner testify to the jury that Betsy was wearing one of the stolen rings. He was now desperate to tie those defendants to the stolen jewelry.

"Mr. Wilson, that seems like a reasonable request to the court – what do you say?"

"Judge – the D.A. demanded to try these three men together – even though we had previously filed a motion to sever the cases because of the likelihood of such a problem occurring. Any evidence linking one particular defendant to this crime would by implication tie the other defendants to the crime, even though the evidence was not relevant to them. The state would need to drop the charges against the other two defendants now before he could introduce this evidence about Betsy's ring. Is he willing to do that?"

The judge grimaced and looked at the prosecutor, "Well, do you want to release the two co-defendants now that double jeopardy has attached – they cannot be tried again?"

"No – I can't release anyone. I want all three convicted so I will charge her but not introduce any evidence concerning that ring," he sighed and we quit for the day.

Everything was now focused on the Georgia Peach's testimony – it was win or lose time for one side or the other. The state, after calling many witnesses, had only proven a burglary and safe cracking had occurred, probably carried out by seasoned professionals. The burglars had worked all day that Sunday, with power tools and cutting torches – cleaning out that jewelry store and no one had suspected or heard a thing.

The three characters I represented were bumbling fools, incapable of such a complex job. They looked more like out of work field hands – professionals at staying in trouble with the law. I suspected the ring drama was just a desperate move by a D.A. facing a town's anger, if he blew this case. There was nothing unique about the small one diamond wedding ring seized by the sheriff. The two so-called eyewitnesses had been reduced to a joke and caused embarrassment to the prosecution.

I spent several hours conferring with the three defendants that night learning everything possible about the Georgia Peach – and a peach of a character she proved to be.

That night, I found an old 8mm movie camera at a local pawnshop. The owner was proud to sell it to me for a few dollars. When court started promptly the next morning, the judge, the prosecutor, and the jurors kept starring at the 8mm movie camera positioned on the counsel table in front of me. Anticipation began building as the G.B.I. agents testified they had been approached by Ms. Peach and informed that she knew who had stolen all the jewelry from a store in Huntsville, Texas, at an earlier burglary.

The agents had confirmed the burglary and obtained search and arrest warrants for the three suspects. The agents said the woman's sworn statement gave them *probable cause* to arrest the three men – which was lawman talk for the real reason for the arrests – the fact that these three men had previous burglary convictions.

The two defendants arrested in Georgia had refused to talk to the agents. The F.B.I. was activated due to the interstate aspects of the case. The remaining suspect was arrested by the Feds in Texas at his wife's home – which was thoroughly searched and nothing of merit found. He also refused to speak to the Agents.

After the state and federal agents testified to their work, it was show time. The D.A. called Ms. Peach to the stand and she opened the courtroom back doors and proudly walked to the witness stand like she was going to meet her groom at the altar. She wore a bright colored dress and high-heel shoes. Her hair was coiffed and she had used plenty of makeup. She smiled innocently at all and took her seat in the witness chair. She was very attractive. The jury watched her closely. She was either the all-American southern lady or a full-fledged harlot – only time would tell.

The D.A. led her through her testimony – starting with her recent enrollment in college in the nursing program. "*She wanted to become a nurse to help people in need. She was twenty-six years old, unmarried and childless. Making her own way in life.*"

She related how she had met Kenneth when she had been forced by circumstances to work in a bar for a while to pay her bills. They began dating and after a few months became very close. Kenneth had introduced her to the two other defendants. They all became such good friends that they even went fishing and camping together on several occasions in the Georgia mountains.

Then she learned that Kenneth was married to a woman in Texas. "I confronted him about being married and he denied it but his friends slipped one day and I learned that he had been lying. They had bragged to me about breaking into the Huntsville jewelry store and I went to the police and told them everything. Kenneth took off for Texas and his two buddies were arrested."

"Do you recognize the three men you described in this courtroom?" – the D.A. asked.

"Yes sir," she sweetly replied. "They are those gentlemen sitting there with that lawyer over there." She pointed to the defendants and glanced down at the movie camera sitting in the center of our counsel table. The blood drained from her face as she looked at me, and then over to the D.A. Her expression changed so much as she stared at that camera that even the D.A. looked over at the camera to see if it was alive.

The D.A. recognized the fear in her eyes, stood up and walked to where his body blocked her view of the camera and defendants and he asked her – "Did you ever see these defendants in possession of a quantity of jewelry?" Another leading question I allowed to pass.

"Yes sir, they showed bags of jewels to me and said they were rich men in the jewelry business." The state passed Ms. Peach for cross-examination.

"Ma'am – are you a movie star?" I asked. A murmur went through the courtroom; everyone's gaze was on my old camera again.

Ms. Peach expression froze, she looked at the D.A. for help – but he was just shuffling his notes. She stared at the old camera for a minute. "Sir, I am not sure what you are asking me?"

"Did these gentlemen ever talk you into appearing in a movie they directed?"

"No sir, I don't know what you are talking about," but her voice had lost its confident sound and she sounded as if she was now on the defensive.

"Ma'am, isn't it true Kenneth filmed you, with your permission, with his eight millimeter camera while you were naked and having sex with both of these other two men?" I pointed to the co-defendants.

"Objection! Not relevant," the D.A. screamed.

"Judge, I will show its relevance with my next question," I replied.

"What is the question, Mr. Wilson?" the judge asked. "Let's don't stray from the reason we are all here."

"Ms. Peach, after you broke up with Kenneth did you demand the movie film back or you would go to the police and have them arrested for making a pornographic movie?"

"Sir!" she replied indignantly. "I don't know what you are talking about. Judge please stop this man from saying these things about me." Her eyes were wide and moist and she was begging the judge to rescue her.

Before the judge could respond – I jumped up, grabbed the camera and held it up in the air. "Judge, since she denies making a dirty movie with these guys and then tried to blackmail them if they did not give her the film – I ask the court's permission to play the movie film for the jury to show them she is perjuring herself."

The courtroom exploded with noise. The D.A. was screaming objections. Ms. Peach was now sobbing with her face in her hands. The courtroom was buzzing in anticipation of watching a dirty movie.

The judge banged his gravel – "Order or I will clear the courtroom. Ma'am, you need to tell the truth or you are going to be in serious trouble, understand?"

"Yes sir, I did allow Kenneth to film me having sex with the other two men. We were all drunk and camping in the woods," she looked down at the floor, avoiding eye contact with anyone. Several jurors were looking at me and shaking their heads.

"Ma'am, did you only go to the G.B.I. with your story when Kenneth refused to give you his movie film?" I asked.

"Yes sir, that is true."

"Did you ask them to give you any of that jewelry that you said they showed you?"

"No sir, why would I do that?" She seemed insulted.

"So, if I understand what you are telling me, you would not lower yourself to ask for stolen jewelry, but you would consent to sex with two men while your boyfriend filmed the little orgy, is that right?"

"Counsel!" The judge spoke up – "I think the jury has got the message – move on."

"One more question, Ma'am, where are you staying while in town and who is paying for it?" I asked and looked at the jury to get their attention.

"I am staying at the Holiday Inn, Room 8. The F.B.I. is paying all the expenses and airfare." She said proudly.

"And who are the two men sleeping in your room each night?"

"Objection!" the D.A shouted as he rose from his chair.

"Overruled," the judge was curious now himself, as well as everyone in the courtroom. "Answer the question, Ma'am."

"The two F.B.I. agents from Georgia," was her innocent reply.

I looked at the jury and they looked at me. It was all over for the state, but the shouting continued for another day.

A day later the case went to the jury after closing arguments and the jury returned in two hours with acquittals for all defendants. It was almost dark when I walked out of the courthouse to my car to drive back to the motel. Two G.B.I. agents were standing nearby smoking.

"Hey Wilson – ever get to Georgia?" – one hollered.

"No reason for me to go," I replied cautiously.

"Come on down, we will take you alligator hunting."

"Sure you will," I said over my shoulder as I drove away.

Were my clients guilty? They said no. I never knew for sure. They were extradited back to Georgia on another unrelated charge.

I was too exhausted to drive the long distance home that night – so after several drinks at the motel lounge I retired to my room for a much needed peaceful and long night's sleep.

At midnight a light knocking on my door awakened me. I was at first concerned that my G.B.I. friends were there for a "gator hunting trip" – but through the peephole I saw Kenneth's wife's face and opened the door – "You O.K.?" I asked.

"Can I spend the night with you? My baby left with his grandparents and I don't want to be alone tonight."

Life is full of surprises.

The jury in Fort Worth had awarded custody of the child to my client, the mother, in my absence – so all was well that ends well.

Doctors are the same as lawyers; the only difference is that lawyers merely rob you, whereas doctors rob and kill you too.
Anton Pavlovich Chekhov

9

A MONTH LATER I RECEIVED A LETTER from the Huntsville D.A. stating his decision to dismiss the criminal case pending against Betsy because of "insufficient evidence," which is lawyer talk for stay the hell away from this courthouse now and forever; which suited me just fine.

I picked up the office phone and called Betsy's father, Zack, where she now lived with her young son to give him the good news and talk about the approaching deer season. He answered and when I informed him of the news he seemed not to understand.

"My Mary died Saturday – heart attack," his voice cracked.

He handed his phone to Betsy who also seemed to be out of sorts. "My sister is dead at twenty-six years old! Her two babies have no mother or father – God damn it all to hell."

I was shaken and at a loss for words. "What happened, Betsy?"

"She died after surgery at the local hospital. The doctor said she died of natural causes – cardiac arrest – or some bullshit. How does a healthy twenty-six year old woman die of cardiac arrest?" Betsy was her usual feisty self, ready to fight a circular saw.

"Did the hospital perform an autopsy," I asked. I heard Betsy holler at her father, "Dad, did they do an autopsy on Mary?"

His booming voice answered, "No, doctor said they cut her to pieces trying to save her life and he didn't see any reason to do further damage to her body. We agreed enough damage was done to her poor body."

"That was a mistake," I moaned over the phone, "Has she been buried?"

"This morning, we just returned from her funeral," Betsy said and I could tell she was not far from losing her composure so I expressed my regrets and apologized for interrupting their family meeting and ended the conversation.

A week later, sixty-five year old Zack and his long-suffering wife of forty years, Grace, sat in my office. They needed legal representation to obtain legal guardianship of Mary's two minor children, aged five and seven years. They had already raised three children, and were now ready to join the growing ranks of grandparents in America that are raising their grandchildren.

The children's father had never married Mary. He had abandoned the family for greener pastures; moved away and wanted no involvement in his two children's lives.

"You folks understand you are going to be responsible for the care and needs of those two kids until they reach eighteen years of age. Are you sure you want that responsibility?" I asked.

"No one else is volunteering, so we have no choice – they are good kids and now they have no one else who cares what happens to them." I could certainly relate to that.

The untimely death of their daughter was bothering me - even though I had never met her, her sudden death seemed suspicious. "Tell me what you know about Mary's hospitalization and death. Why was she in the hospital?"

"She was very vain about her looks. She had bad scars on her stomach from two C-Section births and she wanted to wear a two-piece bathing suit. She wanted those scars removed from her belly. Two days after surgery she suddenly died of cardiac arrest - that's all we know. Her doctors said everyone at the hospital loved her and did all they could to save her – but nothing worked," Grace said.

"Was Mary in a private or semi-private room?" I asked.

"Semi-private, we received a nice card of condolences from the lady who was in the room with Mary when she died – she is such a sweet person – we got to know her when we visited Mary," Grace said.

"Do you have her name and address?" I asked. They thought they did and agreed to furnish it. "I want to look into Mary's death if you will give me your permission?"

They were pleased that I would take the time to do so. It was the least I could do for these good people. They soon found the lady's card and called my secretary. I wrote a letter to the lady who shared Mary's room and requested a few minutes of her time and asked her to call me. She did call and the first words out of her mouth sent chills down my neck.

"They killed her!"

Thirty minutes later I was sitting in her living room. The sixty-eight year old widow told me a story about overhearing a life and death struggle take place between Mary and the hospital staff several hours before Mary went into cardiac arrest that made my blood boil. *They had killed her*. Her story laid the groundwork for what was to be my first wrongful death case. The defendant would be one of the major hospitals in the Fort Worth.

I knew by reputation the hospital's Dallas junkyard dog lawyers and knew they would try their best to chew up an inexperienced young lawyer such as myself. The only wrath worse than a scorned woman is a defense lawyer defending medical malpractice cases. No other type of civil case is harder to win and the vast majority of contested trials end with defendant victories.

The standard of proof required by the courts in medical malpractice cases is very high, and you must have medical experts willing and medically competent in that area of medicine to testify that their fellow medical provider failed to provide your client with the proper standard of medical treatment *and* that failure was the proximate cause of that patient's death, based on reasonable medical probability. Not an easy task for any trial lawyer to perform.

I discussed the pros and cons with Zack and Grace who by now had the legal authority to represent the interests of their grandchildren and the estate of their deceased daughter. They would need all the financial recovery possible to adequately provide the necessities of life for the children and they gave me a green light to proceed.

My first hurdle was to find a qualified medical expert that would be willing to testify the hospital's employees had breached their duty to provide good and proper medical care for the deceased woman. And, most importantly, would he give his medical opinion that the defendant hospital failures proximately caused her death. The burden of proof was on me to show the standard of care and the defendant's failure to conform their treatment to that standard.

A lawyer who decides to handle a medical malpractice case must educate himself on the medical procedures at issue and must know as much or more than the professionals who provided that medical care. Only then will he be able to know when the medical staff involved are telling the truth and prove by expert testimony when they are lying.

The basic facts were not in dispute. Mary had undergone her elective scar repair surgery without incident and was quickly recovering in her hospital room and was two days away from a full discharge. Something happened to her during those two days post-op that killed her. The mystery was what?

Depositions and affidavits from the treating doctors and nurses revealed Mary was recovering nicely and in good spirits with normal vital signs until suddenly her blood pressure started falling rapidly and she went into cardiac arrest and all the king's men and king's horses could not save her life. Her death certificate clearly proclaimed a natural death caused by sudden cardiac arrest, which is doctor-speak for "We bury our mistakes."

The lack of an autopsy was crucial and made my job much harder – from a very hard case to prove to a nearly impossible case to prove.

I developed a time line leading up to her death and a long list of names of each medical provider or employee who had contact with Mary up to the time of her death. I was able to locate and take sworn depositions or statements from every person Mary had contact with, except one person. That person seemed to hold the key to the entire case. She was the nursing student who observed Mary's falling blood pressure readings and reported to the RN on duty the serious danger to Mary's health.

The young nursing student's name was Marie Gomez and she seemed to have vanished after Mary's death. Missing witnesses are not unusual in lawsuits because most people do not want to become "involved" in other people's misfortunes or lawsuits. But, this case was different. I suspected this witness was either in hiding or worse, being hidden by the hospital administration.

A year went by while both sides expended much time and expense trying to defeat the claims of the other with various court motions and hearings. A jury trial date was approaching and a cut off in witness discovery was rapidly approaching and I still could not locate the missing nursing student.

My efforts to find the witness revealed that she had not only quit her job at the hospital after Mary's death, but the young woman had also dropped out of nursing school, even though she was an outstanding student. Her school advisor told me, "Marie said one day she wanted no more of nursing and said she was quitting and moving to San Antonio, Texas, never to return to the profession of nursing." Her advisor gave me the name of the girl's closest classmate. I promised to keep our conversation confidential because the school of nursing was a teaching arm of the hospital we sued.

I quickly located the classmate and girlfriend of Marie and explained to her my urgent need to talk to Marie. "A great injustice is going to occur to two young innocent children of a deceased mother unless I can talk to Marie," I begged. She said she would contact Marie and give her my phone number, but that is all she was willing to do to assist me. "It is up to her if she calls you. She is a very religious person and tries to do the right thing."

Marie did call me – later that day. She called me from a convent in San Antonio, Texas, where she was studying to be a nun.

"I never want anything to do with nursing or medicine again," she blurted. The story she told forever changed my view of hospital care. I would never be comfortable visiting a hospital again.

I heard her draw a deep breath and she began: "I was assigned to the eleven to seven shift – the grave yard shift. Nobody wanted to work that shift. When I came on duty that night – one of my duties was to check the vitals on all the post-operative patients on my floor. I had become friendly with Mary, she was a sweet woman recovering from scar surgery and had a nasogastric tube in place at all times to drain away excess fluids and gases that built up in her stomach following abdominal surgery. We call it a NG tube; it is inserted in one nostril down the throat into the stomach."

"When I first checked her vitals that night she was fine and asleep. But, she pulled on her NG tube during her sleep and it needed to be reinserted in order to function properly. I reported the NG tube problem to the RN on duty – not one of my favorite people - and I heard her call to the intern on duty to come help her with the patient in Room 1214 – *that damn cry-baby has pulled out her NG tube, again.*"

"The three of us went to Mary's room and I pulled the privacy curtains so not to disturb the other woman patient. The intern told the RN to hold Mary's head and shoulders down and he forced the NG tube back down Mary's nose. That woke Mary and she tried to pull the tube back out and a struggle began with the intern and RN pushing the tube down and Mary trying to pull it out."

"I knew from experience that the tube needed to be completely removed and Mary needed to cooperate with its insertion. They strapped Mary down with her screaming and fighting and they sedated her and she passed out. She never woke up again."

"I noticed Mary's blood pressure started dropping and reported it to the RN who just blew me off. Mary's blood pressure soon reached a dangerous level at four o'clock in the morning and the RN still refused to call Mary's doctor so I did, knowing that was probably the end of my nursing career. The doctor was furious and demanded to speak with the RN."

"The doctor told the RN to take Mary to ICU immediately and he was on the way. Two minutes later Mary went into cardiac arrest before we could even transport her to the ICU."

"They did everything they could to revive her but she was dead. When the doctor arrived he told everyone to keep their mouths shut about the matter, that the NG tube had probably punctured Mary's stomach and she had developed massive sepsis throughout her body."

"I quit my job on the spot, and never went back."

My mind was racing, "Marie, one more question and I will let you go – I know you aren't a doctor, but what do you think happened to Mary? Her hospital roommate heard everything going on and told me. 'They *killed Mary.*' What do you believe happened to Mary," I asked.

"I suspect, when they did not fully remove the NG tube as they should have and reinserted it – they ruptured her stomach with the end of the tube and she was slowly dying of sepsis from the ruptured contents of her stomach." She continued, "When Mary's blood pressure started dropping they should have recognized her trauma and taken her to ICU and surgery immediately."

I heard Marie's slight sigh over phone, like a great weight had been lifted. I thanked Marie after getting her address and phone number in case I had to subpoena her.

The next day I called Mary's treating doctor whom I had not named as a defendant in the lawsuit and told him that he needed to contact his lawyer and the three of us needed to meet before I had to join the good doctor as a party-defendant. "I have found the missing witness, the nursing student – and will be naming her as a witness in the case." I briefly related to him her version of what had occurred concerning Mary's death.

The doctor and his lawyer met with me the next afternoon. Everyone was quite nervous and knew the stakes had risen considerably for all involved in this matter with this newly discovered evidence.

I told the doctor my theory of Mary's death, which was basically the same story Marie had told and asked him and his lawyer; "Doctor, are you willing to testify that Mary's probable cause of death was massive sepsis and contamination in her body from the rupture of her stomach by the improper insertion of the NG tube and that if she had received good medical care, she would have been immediately taken to surgery when her vital signs showed she was in life-threatening distress? Otherwise, I am going to name you as a co-defendant since you clearly participated in the hospital's cover-up of the real cause of Mary's death."

He agreed to testify on our behalf. I supplemented our list of witnesses with the good doctor's and Marie's names and amended our trial pleadings to include the new revelations concerning the NG tube and the case was eventually set for trial.

The lawyers for the hospital invited me for lunch at the firm's private club on the top floor of a Dallas skyscraper and presented me with a fair offer of settlement which would provide a generous monthly income to the two minor children until they each reached the age of twenty-five. Of course, the grandparents and I also recovered a generous amount as approved by the court.

This would not be my last medical malpractice case, but it was an eye-opening experience for me of the dangers in the medical care field. I also learned firsthand where those terms: *practicing* law and *practicing* medicine originated.

But for the concerned lady patient who was Mary's roommate – the actual circumstances of this untimely death would have simply been buried with Mary, forever.

When Zack and his wife came to my office to pick up their settlement check – they brought their crippled neighbor, Sam, with them.

It seemed that Sam was impressed with the favorable outcome Zack's family had received and he wanted me to represent him on "his" medical malpractice injury. Sam had talked to several lawyers who had declined to represent him, so he had given up until Zack had suggested he talk to me – since I was a miracle worker and walked on water.

Sam and Zack were both old oil field rough necks whose bodies had endured much damage over the years. Almost two years earlier Sam had finally agreed to back surgery when his deteriorating back was causing him endless pain.

His back surgery at the leading local hospital had gone fine and he was one day post-op when suddenly his left leg began to "rot away," as he explained it. Sam then stood and dropped his pants to show me firsthand the horrible remains of his left thigh. It was nothing but scar tissue, a big hole, and an almost naked leg bone between his knee and his hip. I almost gagged and turned my face away.

"Wow, what happened?" I inquired.

"It was one day after my surgery and I was asleep and all of a sudden my left thigh started burning. I thought someone was running a hot poker through my leg. I had a back brace on and could not move and I started screaming. They shot me full of morphine and I passed out. Over the next few days all the skin on my left leg between my knee and hip rotted and fell away – I was left with just a huge hole where my thigh used to be. No one could explain to me what happened. To this day the hospital has stonewalled me as to what happened to my leg, which had nothing to do with my back surgery."

Another mindbender of a case lay at my feet for the taking – as if I needed more hard cases to try to prove in a courtroom. I told Sam to leave his medical records for me to review and I would get back to him in a few days.

A thorough review of Sam's medical records revealed he had undergone routine fusion surgery on his lumbar spine and was in a normal post-op recovery period, under heavy sedation, when he had been administered a very strong pain killer injection in his left thigh. His charts revealed immediate adverse reaction with extensive tissue damage and loss. His doctor's reported diagnosis showed he had suffered permanent loss of skin and muscle to his left thigh.

The hospital ignored my written demand for compensation for Sam – and with his whole-hearted approval a lawsuit for negligence was soon filed contending negligence in the administration of the injection into his left thigh. The hospital and their bulldogs made no offer of compromise so the battle lines formed before an empaneled jury to determine if medical negligence had occurred once again.

I had secured an excellent doctor of toxicology to testify the particular pain killer that had been administered to Sam had to be injected deep into the thigh muscle or it could cause great tissue loss and burns to the surrounding skin tissue. And, in his medical opinion, "The nurse that administered the injection must have not injected the pain killer deep enough into the thigh muscle and the faulty injection had been the proximate cause of the great tissue loss and burns suffered by Sam."

I then called as a witness, the chief of staff and chief surgeon of the hospital we sued. The judge and defense lawyers looked at each other and grinned – they and I knew this doctor was famous for hating plaintiff lawyers and testifying for the defense in medical malpractice cases. There were puzzled as to why I would place an obviously hostile expert witness on the stand.

"Doctor – this patient's chart states that he suffered an *adverse reaction* to the particular pain killer that was administered into his left thigh. Is that your professional opinion also, relying on the treatment this man received at your hospital?"

"Yes, there is no doubt that occasionally a person – for reasons that no one can explain – will react in an adverse way to a particular medication – there is no way we can guard against, or predict, when and to whom such an adverse reaction will occur. In my professional opinion, that is what occurred in this case and no personnel was negligent in injecting this patient – it was one of those one out of a thousand cases where a patient just has an adverse reaction," the doctor explained and warmly smiled at the impressed jury.

"Doctor, isn't there one way to test a patient first to make sure they do not react violently to a particular medication – which might harm them?" I asked.

"Well, yes – I guess you could give them a small dose of the medication and watch for any adverse reaction in the patient," the doctor said, "But that was not done in this instance."

"And why was that not done in this case with this patient?" I asked and handed the witness the patient's post-op medical chart.

"Because he received an injection of the same pain killer six hours earlier with no reactions or problems."

The doctor's face immediately paled and he looked at the two defense lawyers for help – they looked back helplessly. The judge looked at me and I looked at the jury and they looked at each other. The trial was essentially over.

The doctor was then excused to leave – knowing that his offhand comments had single-handedly won our case for us. There had been no adverse reaction – only a negligent injection.

I never tried any more medical malpractice cases after those two – I referred all new cases to law firms that specialized in such cases. The practice of medical malpractice law was evolving into a firm specialty – both on the plaintiffs and defendants side of the bar. It was not an area for a non-specialist to tread.

Sam was fairly compensated by the jury – they awarded every penny I had requested in my pleadings and my closing argument. The jury understood the embarrassment Sam had to carry for the remainder of his life of a disfigured leg that would prevent him from ever wearing a bathing suit or shorts in a public area.

After the trial was over and court officially adjourned and my grateful client had left the courthouse – I was approached by several of the members of the jury – they had a question for me. "Why didn't you ask for more money? We were prepared to award your client much more damages then you requested."

I was speechless for a moment, but finally managed to say – "My client only wanted reasonable damages – he knew the nurse just made a simple mistake," was my embarrassed reply.

"Simple mistake! She almost killed him," replied one of the jurors.

I thanked them again for their verdict and quickly left the courthouse. I had just made a simple mistake myself – one I never made again. Thereafter, I always plead for, and demanded more, damages than I could reasonable expect a judge or jury to award. Let them make the final determination.

Justice, n.
A commodity which is a more or less adulterated condition
the state sells to the citizen as a reward for his
allegiance, taxes and personal service.
The Devil's Dictionary.

10

No legal system of criminal justice is perfect. Our society has gone from simple to complex. We started with the four common law crimes: Murder – Robbery – Assault and Rape. We have *progressed and* evolved to a statutory scheme of thousands of criminal offenses. The government's circle of laws and prosecutions grows even larger each day.

Sometimes a unique set of facts occurs and the legal system goes haywire. It happened to me. It happened to Mary Squires.

Mary's big sin was she loved dogs, and in particular, the breed of hunting dogs known as Weimaraners. I had never even heard of a Weimaraner; that all changed early one morning at my office before I could drink my first cup of life giving caffeine.

I heard the big man before I saw him. "They killed them all! I need to see Wilson, now."

I heard my receptionist ask George to please sit down.

I walked out to the waiting room to assist and extended my hand to the obviously upset man who looked to be in his mid-sixties, dressed like a farmer.

"Who killed who?" I asked, my concern growing as I looked at George's disheveled clothes and the dirt and dried blood covering his overalls.

"They killed all the dogs!" He fairly spat the words out as he followed me into my office.

"Sir, – you need to talk lower and have a seat – take a deep breath and start at the beginning so I can take notes." My voice had an edge to it and he bowed his head and dropped like a sack of cow feed into a chair in front of my desk.

"It reminded me of what I saw in the big war – when my unit liberated one of those death camps in Germany – big holes full of bodies. I never thought I would see the day that happened in America," George's lower lip started to quiver and his eyes moistened.

"Please start at the beginning, so I can get my head wrapped around what happened." My voice was lower now with a touch of empathy. George was obviously very shaken about what occurred, but I needed a starting point so I could get a grip on the situation. After all, three years of law school was for the purpose of training lawyers' minds to focus on the legal issues raised by a very convoluted set of confusing facts.

George quieted down and related the background story on Mary and her dog business. He and Mary were neighbors and shared a love of dogs – especially hunting hounds. Mary was a widow with no family. George was a widower with no family. Those dogs became the center of their attention and Mary's reason for living.

"Mary is famous on a national scale for her show dogs – and she is often mentioned in national kennel magazines for her pure breed Weimaraners. Several years ago she purchased ten acres of rural farmland to build her large kennel business and invested her life's savings in the thing. It grew and her business expanded faster than she could keep up with it and she relied on me and several other volunteers to help her feed and water her many dogs. She was on duty every hour of the day, with no breaks or vacations. Last week she drove her truck to Fort Worth to buy dog food and she suffered a near fatal heart attack at the feed store and has been in a coma ever since."

George continued, "It all started when one of Mary's kennel customers came out to the kennel to pick up her dog that Mary was training – the old busy-body could not find Mary or anyone out there and called the Sheriff and told them there must be foul play involved, Mary has disappeared," George took a breath.

"The Sheriff could not find anyone at the kennel and called the local humane society office and reported the animals were abandoned." George's chin started quivering again – and I braced myself for more emotional outbursts – they came quickly.

"The humane society manager and his crew came out and made a hasty decision the kennel had been abandoned and there was no way the owner could care for over one hundred fifty hound dogs so they called their vet in Fort Worth and directed him to come out and put down the dogs," George put his trembling hands to his face and continued.

"I heard the dogs barking and saw all the strange cars and I drove over and asked them *what the hell is going on* and they had the Sheriff escort me down the road. I was screaming at them that I would feed and water the dogs and they didn't need to kill them. No one knew then that Mary was in the hospital in a coma. We didn't learn that until later that day when the hospital called the kennel phone asking for the name of Mary's next of kin. They thought she was dying," George was talking and almost sobbing now.

"I called the other volunteers and we all went to Mary's kennel and told those people about Mary and that we would care for the dogs until Mary returned – but it was too late. They had brought in a tractor and backhoe and dug a big trench about twenty feet long and ten feet deep and dumped all those dead dogs into that trench and we watched that tractor dump dirt into that trench until it was completely filled and then all of them packed up their shit and drove away – like nothing had even happened. We were all in shock and sick to our stomachs."

"How many dogs do you estimate they killed?" I asked my mind struggling to comprehend and thinking, *this can't be true – this is America.*

"About one hundred fifty dogs – some of them were puppies. All registered purebreds."

"How did they kill them?" I asked, wondering how they could have killed so many dogs so quickly.

"There was a vet and his two helpers with syringes and they would inject their poison into the dog's chest and the dog would just collapse with its legs kicking. The killers went from cage to cage quickly like burglars working. Then they just threw the dead dogs in the front end loader of their tractor and it carried the dogs to the big hole and dumped them." George was now wrung out and trembling.

"Why didn't they just let you and your friends care for the dogs? Why the need to kill all of them so quickly?" I asked.

"They said they had a court order to destroy all the animals and that anyone that interfered was going to jail," George looked at me and waited for me to solve this terrible mess.

I thought a moment – wondering how the killers had managed to get a court order to kill Mary's animals without allowing her due process of law – due notice and a fair hearing. Obviously, Mary's rights were not a great concern to some judge or these people.

"George, what is it you want me to do about all this – the dogs belong to Mary and she is in a coma. Why did you come to see me?" I asked.

George's eyes widened – "Oh! I didn't tell you the worse part – it gets better." I braced myself for the *really* bad news.

"There is a warrant out for Mary's arrest for animal cruelty. We took up a collection to pay you to defend her." George held out a wad of small bills. I pushed his hand away.

"Keep your money George, Mary may not survive – so let's wait and see what happens to her. Are you going to look after her farm?" I asked.

"Yes, I am feeding and watering her other livestock and everything is being taken care of for the time being. It will be awhile before the doctors will know if Mary is going to make it."

"O.K., George, when and if Mary recovers, tell her I will make her bail bond and defend her. Stay in touch and she is lucky to have such a good friend as you."

A month later, George returned, with a defeated and fragile looking Mary in tow. They took their seats in my office. There was more to this story than I had heard from George. I knew Texas law required that an animal's owner must be given notice and an opportunity to appear in the local Justice Court before the owner's animals could be destroyed, for any reason. There was one exception – the Justice of the Peace could order immediate destruction in an emergency. With my client watching and listening I reached for my phone and call the Justice of the Peace who would have jurisdiction over Mary's case. Luckily the judge answered her own phone that day.

"Judge, this is Bob Wilson – did you give permission to the local humane society to kill all of Mary Squire's hound dogs?"

There was a long pause on the phone and then a weak voice asked, "Why do you ask?"

"Because I heard you did and that Mary Squire has been charged with animal cruelty," I waited for her reply.

"The vet said the dogs were all dying of heartworms and needed to be put down immediately, I had no choice, he was the expert."

"Did you go out and see for yourself," I asked.

Another long pause – "No, no need to – I know nothing about dogs and they're the experts."

"Did you know the owner was in a coma from a heart attack she suffered that morning when you signed your Order?"

Another long pause – "No, they told me the dogs were abandoned!" her voice fading and uneasy. Suddenly she spoke up – "Got to go." Click.

I looked at George and Mary who had overheard both sides of the conversation. He was shaking his head and becoming angry, again.

"George, how often did you visit Mary's kennel?" I asked.

"Everyday – I helped her feed and clean the kennels. It was getting too much for her."

"Mary, what kind of health were your dogs in when you had your heart attack?" I asked.

"They were well fed and watered. Several had heartworms – but were being treated. There was no reason to kill them." Her voice cracked and tears ran down her cheeks as she put her hands to her face.

"Mary, how are you doing health wise?"

"I am weak, and my heart is broken – those dogs were my whole life. They kept me alive and were my family."

"Mary, you are charged with animal cruelty. The county attorney in Cleburne wants you to plead guilty. They will agree to a two year probated sentence and one thousand dollar fine," I said and watched for her reaction.

She seemed to melt into my overstuffed leather chair. The final indignity – they killed and destroyed everything she lived for and now they wanted their pound of flesh.

George spoke first – "It will be a cold day in hell before Mary pleads guilty – she did nothing wrong," he wrapped his big arm around her sagging shoulders.

"I suspect the county attorney is worried about the county's liability in this case. If they can get a criminal conviction, it will be difficult for you to recover any damages from the county," I said.

I already knew the bad publicity released by the local media forever destroyed what little chance Mary had of rebuilding her business. That also had the effect of poisoning the pool of potential jurors in her criminal case.

"Mr. Wilson, I have no money to pay you. I am completely broke, I cannot even raise five hundred dollars to post my bail bond," Mary's eyes moistened again.

"Mary, I will make your bond and represent you in court at no charge. Someday give me one of your hound dogs. I am a hunter and would like to have one."

Mary smiled for the first time – glad to know I was on her side and also wanted to have one of her pets.

Six months later we were called to trial against overwhelming odds. The state called the vet who testified all the destroyed dogs had severe cases of heartworms.

"I reported my findings to the Justice of the Peace and she ordered me to destroy all the animals. So, I was following her orders."

The Justice of the Peace testified that she was informed the owner had abandoned the animals and there was no one to care for them and the vet said they were all going to die from worms. "I signed a destroy order."

The officials from the humane society testified: "We just followed the vet and the Judge's directives and did the humane thing and put the animals down, since they would have starved to death anyway since there was no one caring for the dogs."

No one seemed to remember who had the idea to dig the mass grave for the dogs and gave that order.

George described the scene better than anyone when he testified: "They were all Nazis carrying out their orders to kill and bury, with no one accepting any responsibility."

Mary tried to testify but kept breaking down in tears. She said all her dogs were being cared for as "Best she could and yes, some had heartworms, but were being treated."

The jury found Mary guilty of animal cruelty – i.e., animal neglect. They assessed the minimum sentence and probated that. The jury was not proud of their verdict and avoided eye contact with anyone as they marched out of the courtroom. The prosecutor smiled. The judge looked at me and shook his head in disbelief of the guilty verdict. I was disgusted with the whole system.

The injustice train pulled away from the station that day – much like those trains full of frightened Jews back in Hitler's days. Everyone simply followed orders and no one accepted any responsibility for their actions – going along to get along with the authorities, and the locals backed them up with their verdict.

Every citizen must always stand tall when called upon to administer justice to his fellow citizen; and, standing tall does not necessarily mean to carry out the commands of some governmental authority. Blind faith in authority is the end of justice – not the beginning. As Lord Acton said: "Power corrupts and absolute power corrupts absolutely." It is no defense to injustice that one just followed orders. At least, that is what America told the Germans at the Nuremberg trials.

In 1940, the United State's Attorney General, Robert Jackson gave a speech in which he stated:

"The Prosecutor has more control over life, liberty and reputation than any other person in America. He can have citizens investigated, and if he is that kind of person, he can have this done to the tune of public statements and veiled or unveiled intimidations...While the prosecutor at his best is one of the beneficent forces in our society, when he acts from malice or other base motives, he is one of the worst."

The average lawyer is essentially a mechanic who
Works with a pen instead of a ball peen hammer.
Robert Schmitt

11

A MIDDLE-AGED BROTHER/SISTER TEAM PRESENTED A PUZZLE to me one morning concerning the recent deaths of both their parents. The local medical examiner had signed death certificates for the old couple, both of whom were almost seventy years old: "death by natural causes."

"O.K., I'm sorry for your recent loss but what is the problem?" I replied.

It seemed that the couple had been found dead in their bed one morning by my new clients when they failed to return phone calls or answer their door for two days. The idea that an old couple could both die the same night, in the same bed, of natural causes did seem a little strange.

I asked the clients in detail about the health of their parents. "They had issues with blood pressure, aches and pains in their joints, and chronic constipation," they replied. Those ailments were fairly common for a couple of their age.

There was no question of suicide, or a murder-suicide event. The deceased couple had died over a month earlier. And, as usual – no autopsy had been done and the bodies had since been cremated. I remembered the similar facts of the hospital death of the young vain mother.

"How convenient, does it get any better?" was my sarcastic response, I was getting a little impatient with people bringing me impossible cases to try to win for them.

The brother/sister team had talked to numerous lawyers about their concerns, but no lawyer was interested in looking into the matter and they could not afford to pay a lawyer on an hourly or retainer basis to investigate this case.

I asked them if they had made a thorough search of their dead parents' home, which by chance had not been touched since the medical examiner's investigation was concluded. Their reply was the first item of good luck: "We have not, but need to, since it is about to be placed on the market for sale by the probate judge – here are the keys."

I had them sign a contingent fee contract with our office. I suggested some type of cover-up had occurred but we needed strong evidence to support my theory.

I sent my investigator with the clients to do a thorough search of the house with instructions to look for anything suspicious and bag it, photograph it and label it with information of where they found the items in the house. To everyone's surprise, when they looked behind the headboard of the deceased couple's double bed, they found a fistful of drugstore computer printouts revealing hundreds of prescription purchases of painkiller drugs. The printouts revealed the names of the drug stores. What caught my investigator and my immediate interest was the printouts revealed numerous purchases of the same prescription painkillers being purchased on a *daily basis* by the dead couple. There was no way two people could consume that many prescription painkillers daily and have lived even one week without dying of an overdose.

It was obvious that something unlawful was afoot. The illegal sale of prescription painkillers is a nasty business and widespread in this Country. Usually big money and influential people are involved. It is also dangerous ground for the unwary to tread.

I swore everyone involved to secrecy and emphasized "This was serious business and potentially a dangerous situation for all involved. We now have proof that the dead couple probably died from overdoses of prescription painkillers but we have no medical proof, yet. We must have medical experts to prove our case."

I knew from past case investigations that there was a little known state regulation requiring all funeral homes to draw a blood sample from all dead bodies before that body was cremated or embalmed and keep the blood for a certain period of time. I held my breath and called the funeral home where the old couple had been cremated and inquired about whether the blood samples still existed.

They did! What a break. I was told "There is a small amount of blood drawn from each body and it was kept in our refrigerator since the cremation." I sent my investigator *post haste* to get the two capsules of blood with an authorization and release signed by my clients, the only surviving children.

I called a professor of toxicology at a local medical school and retained him to run tests on the two capsules of blood and also sent him copies of the drugstore printouts we had discovered in the bedroom and a basic outline of what we had discovered so far in our investigation.

The next day he called me back and confirmed my suspicions – "There are lethal levels of prescription painkillers in both blood samples." The doctor's toxicology findings raised serious questions about the medical examiner's reports and the doctor who signed the two death certificates of natural causes.

These facts also raised questions about the subject drug stores, which were owned by the same wealthy family. Why did those drug stores fill prescriptions of massive doses of painkillers to this old couple in the first place? And to further complicate the picture, the prescribing doctor on all the hundreds of prescriptions had signed the couple's death certificates. He was also the dead couple's longtime treating doctor.

I called and made an appointment with the deceased couple's doctor. He was not happy to see me and seemed very uncomfortable, appearing anxious and hurried. "I am very busy and really do not have time for this. What seems to be the problem?" He did not attempt to hide his disdain for me and probably for lawyers in general.

I ceased all pretenses of being a fellow professional and cut to the chase. I handed the good doctor a copy of the many pages of printout prescriptions, which clearly showed him as the prescribing doctor. His face turned white and then bright red. "I did not write these prescriptions." The plot thickened. The doctor sat down at his desk, his hands starting to shake.

In response to my further questions he replied: "Yes, I was treating the couple for heart issues and joint pains and arthritis. But, I would never have prescribed them this many pain medications."

"Why is that doctor - would it have killed them?" I increased the pressure.

"Probably, but no two people could have consumed all these drugs, it is impossible. They would have had to take hundreds of pills per day. That would have been lethal."

The doctor suddenly realized that I could be his best friend or worse enemy if these matters became public. I suspected he knew much more about this situation than he wanted me to know.

"What can I do to assist you," he asked, his entire demeanor now fully changed.

"Just testify to the truth, that you did not write these prescriptions," I said, looking directly into his eyes – both of us knowing that he would never tell the *whole* truth. "And, that these daily amounts of prescribed medications would be lethal to this old couple."

I took my leave, wishing I was a fly on the wall that could stay and listen to the phone calls he was about to make after I was gone. But, I could clearly hear that conversation in my mind – "Cover your ass, this S.O.B. knows!"

I investigated the drug stores involved. They were moneymaking operations, the busiest drug stores in town - they were owned by two brothers who were licensed pharmacists and were quite wealthy and very politically active. Both men currently held politically important elective positions. They donated generously to certain local politicians and judicial campaigns. They also kept the local power lawyers on retainer. I would be taking on the so-called establishment if I proceeded to trial on this case.

I paid a visit to the local medical examiner and showed him the toxicology reports from my expert witness. He too, was not happy to see me. He could not remember why he failed to do blood tests on the old couple.

"They appeared to have expired from natural causes when I examined them in their beds, no sign of foul play and I saw no need to do toxicology tests," was his shaky response.

I began to suspect the M.E., the treating doctor, and the owners of the drug stores were all involved in a criminal conspiracy because of the one question that each suspect always asked me: "Where did you get that printout of prescription drugs those people were taking?" That seemed to be their greatest concern and, was quite a mystery in itself.

That printout of filled prescriptions this couple had obtained was the key to this case and somehow they had obtained it from the very drug stores that killed them. Strangely, no empty pill containers for the particular drugs that killed them were found in the dead couple's home. Only non-lethal pill containers were found. Someone cleaned up the evidence, but missed the most important item.

The mystery of who stuck all those drug stores printouts behind the dead couple's headboard was never solved, but that did not matter because the drug stores' owners never denied it was their printouts when I took their depositions. They only denied their direct involvement.

We filed suit against the drug stores and their owners. I was shocked to learn they never bothered to incorporate their businesses – they owned them individually, along with their big homes and fat bank accounts. They were too tight with their ample funds to incorporate their drug business.

I would have, and wanted to, sue the dead couple's treating doctor and the medical examiner, but it would have made my job much harder since they could just play dumb and dumber. It would be more difficult to prove malpractice on their behalf and prove they actually *caused or contributed in some way* to the deaths. I needed the treating doctor's cooperation that he did not prescribe those killer drugs and the M.E.'s cooperation that the dead couple had died from lethal drug overdoses.

The pharmacists hired several well-connected law firms to defend them. In their depositions they, "Couldn't understand how all those prescriptions managed to get filled without them noticing. They disputed that many prescriptions were filled at their drug stores and that it was all the result of a computer error creating the printout."

The day of trial arrived and everyone trooped to the courthouse. The court clerk began interviewing the large jury panel of local citizens in preparation for jury selection.

The babel of defense attorneys motioned me into the empty jury room. Their appointed lead counsel quietly shut the door. "Wilson, are you really going to go through with this trial? You will only succeed in ruining my clients' good name."

"I will let the jury decide if they deserve to keep their good names," I replied.

The gray-headed, pillar of the legal community then said, "Okay – let's quit the small talk. What will it take for this matter to just go away, forever? Keep in mind, my clients' liability insurance carrier will not pay anything or even defend my clients because this is an intentional tort case and my clients are paying everything out of their own pockets," he was now asking me for sympathy.

"That's good," I said. "They should all be indicted by a grand jury, but we both know that will not happen, being the pillars of the community that they are," I said mockingly. "Aren't they both on the board of directors of that Bank across the street?"

"Yes, why do you ask," – their lawyer inquired.

"Because they have thirty minutes to go over to that bank and bring a cashier's check made out to my clients and me for one million dollars – or get ready to have their butts roasted in that courtroom," my expression made clear I was not kidding.

"Okay, let me talk to them – stay right here."

He was back in ten minutes with an associate in tow – he wanted a witness to our next conversation. "They will have to cash some bonds and will need thirty days – they will accept your settlement and tender a cashier check to you now for two hundred thousand dollars," and they did – done deal – case settled.

The questions remained unanswered concerning what did the dead couple do with hundreds of prescription pain pills per day that they supposedly purchased? I believe in actuality the couple received far fewer pills than these computer records listed and the drug stores were simply billing their insurance company and the state and federal government for thousands of dollars for medicines that were never dispensed. It was a criminal enterprise, feeding several greedy entities.

There was no evidence the couple were dealing drugs or passing pills to anyone else. The dead couple certainly took heavy doses of painkillers to the point they lost touch with reality and both died from the steady buildup of lethal chemicals in their bodies.

I can only suspect that someone in the know in one of the drug stores delivered the damning evidence of a criminal conspiracy to the deceased couple one day. The old couple must have stuck it behind their bedpost, either knowingly or in a drug induced stupor, for someone to later find.

Drug stores have strict reporting requirements on the prescription drugs they receive and dispense. The printout we discovered would have surely triggered an official investigation, unless, as I suspect, there were two sets of records kept by the drug stores – one set for the governmental agencies and another set for the internal use only of the owners – that was the copy we had found and it was a lethal dosage in itself for all concerned.

Law students are trained in the case method, and to the lawyer everything in life looks like a case.
Edward Packard, Jr.

12

ONE OF THE MOST STRESSFUL AND UNCOMPROMISING cases a lawyer can handle is a child custody case. The rules of civil discourse go out the window and you are constantly amazed that two parents who once swore to love and cherish each other forever are now trying to inflict the coup de grace on the other marriage partner by *getting* their child or children. As if anyone can really *take* another human being away from one of its parents.

Most lawyers avoid divorce and custody cases like the plague after they have handled several contested cases. By that time most of their clients have discovered, to their great chagrin, that dividing up the children and assets results in both the parties now having less than they once had. There are no winners, only losers, in a divorce or child custody cases and the lawyers involved usually get blamed for everything by everyone after the dust settles. But, young lawyers must eat and keep their doors open, so they take cases they dislike until hopefully one day that really big case comes along and they can retire and do something they really enjoy with their lives.

One day I was blessed or cursed, depending on your point of view, with being retained on two separate child custody cases on the same day. When I arrived at work at seven o'clock in the morning a young man was sitting in his pickup truck outside my office half asleep. I asked him if he was alright since my office was not open and he replied, "If you are willing to talk to me, I will be fine. I just got off work and wanted to speak to you before going home."

I ushered Jimmy into my darkened office and turned on the lights and made coffee.

"We usually require clients to make appointments," I said, trying to make sure he understood this meeting was not going to become a pattern for the future.

"I know, I apologize, but I have been slowly losing my mind and did not know which way to turn. Even my preacher was of no help when I asked."

With two steaming cups of coffee now sitting on my desk I asked him to "Try to get to the point, since I needed to work on some other pressing matters".

"My wife is *up to something* – I just don't know what or how she is doing it. I need your legal advice." The expression on his face told me he was sincere and he was at his wits-end.

"I have three beautiful daughters which I love dearly. They mean the whole world to me – couldn't live without them; that's why I want to hire you."

"So what's the problem?" I said, hoping he would get to the point.

"My wife is always too tired for sex with me and that makes me think she has a boyfriend. I don't know how she manages to see him because she stays home with our three small girls every day and she doesn't drive or go anywhere during the day."

I could see the conversation was going nowhere, so I asked, "What hours and days do you work?"

"Graveyard, eleven until six thirty in the morning – Monday through Friday at the local Miller brewing plant," he replied. "We all go to church on Sunday and I take my wife shopping each Saturday, she is always home."

I was feeling a bit impatient. I needed to end this conversation politely and get him out of my office. I leaned forward, looking him straight in his eyes. "O.K., look – this is the deal – your wife is probably having her boyfriend over on the nights you work, after she puts the girls to bed. I suggest you talk to your boss at work and tell him your lawyer needs you to take some photographs at one o'clock in the morning. You go purchase a Polaroid camera with a flashcube and some color film and tonight slip into your house quietly and without turning on any lights or making any noise. Walk into your bedroom and take four flash photos of your wife as fast as possible and then turn and leave without saying a word. Bring me those four photos when you get off work tomorrow morning."

He looked at me with a shocked expression and stood, "What if she isn't doing anything?"

I stood and held out my hand, "Then you have nothing to worry about, do you. If she *is* doing something – don't say or do anything – get out of there fast."

I ushered him out of the front door thinking I would probably never see him again and I focused on more pressing matters.

At one o'clock that afternoon a well-dressed and clearly depressed thirty-four year old woman arrived for her appointment to retain my services on her divorce case, her husband had already filed for divorce. She introduced herself, Joann – a registered nurse and then she broke down and cried for effect. After she had my attention, she went through two handfuls of tissues and shared with me the details of a twelve-year loveless marriage to a heartless engineer who treated her like a brainless slave.

Since Texas is a no-fault divorce state I wasn't sure why the need for all the vitriol until she uttered those magic and expensive words, "He wants custody of my babies." The tears started again. I tried to reassure her, "It's very difficult for a man to obtain custody of minor children, I am sure you have nothing to worry about," I said in a comforting voice – knowing that divorcing parties frequently use that threat as a bargaining tool.

"I tried to kill myself – is that going to be a problem?" She watched for my reaction. My smile quickly faded, "Better tell me what happened, *that* could be a real issue," I said and watched her more closely. Suddenly I knew this was not going to be the usual divorce case and I wasn't sure I wanted to be involved - a crying woman is one thing, a suicidal woman is another. People going through a divorce are usually irrational enough without the additional problem of suicide attempts.

An attempted suicide by a party who wants custody of their children creates an issue as to their fitness to have custody of minor children. Attempted suicide is prima-facie proof of emotional instability of a parent. I could tell Joann was embarrassed to have to explain the episode, which made me think that she realized her type of behavior has no place in a child custody court battle.

"My husband, John, has been belittling me and running me down for several years, he constantly tells me I look and dress horribly and he refuses to take me anywhere. He says I can't even boil water and I'm worthless in bed."

The tears started flowing again. "He wanted no sex with me and he would get a Playboy magazine and whack-off on the corner of the bed at night all the while making wise-cracks and running me down. He is a very sick, but very smart man."

I had learned by then that women in distress are always freely discussing their sex lives much more than their husbands, who seem to think such matters, are private, even in a divorce setting. Joann was an attractive woman, but the months of depression had taken a toll on her.

I brought her a glass of water and she continued. "He does not smoke, drink, spend money or chase women, *he is perfect* or so he says and thinks. He is as cold as an icebox and has no compassion for our kids or me. They act like little robots around him and they hardly speak at all in his presence. They are afraid to upset him."

"Tell me about your children, who do they prefer to live with?" I asked trying to change the subject.

"They are eight and ten years old. My son is the oldest. He is a sweetheart and both want to stay with me and John knows that, so he wants custody, just to show me he is still the boss – even after we are divorced."

Due to their young age, under Texas law, they would not be allowed to designate their primary custody parent.

I spent the next hour questioning Joann in detail about her relationship with engineer John. Both parents were well educated, well paid, with good work histories. Neither had any harmful habits that stood out. The two children were bright and well-adjusted and they lived in a nice house with all the necessities of life. The only family problem seemed to be that John was a control freak.

"John started putting a lot of pressure on me two years ago to leave him and the children and just go away, said he didn't want to have to look at me anymore. I tried to be the perfect wife, but nothing worked. He tried, and succeeded, in making my life very miserable. He encouraged me to take tranquilizers and sedatives I could easily get at my work. He says the pills made me easier to live with when I am a space cadet." The tears started again.

"Tell me in detail about the suicide thing," I asked and waited for the details of what I already knew was going to be the main issue in this custody case.

She took a deep breath and started. "I normally have each Wednesday off from work. I got up that morning and prepared breakfast and packed lunches for John and the two children and stayed up until they were gone to work and school. The children caught the school bus and when John walked out the door he turned and said: 'why don't you just do all of us a favor and take *all* your pills this morning'. Then he slammed the door and squealed his tires down the driveway."

"I sat down on my bed and cried for a while. I still had my robe on since I had planned to go back to sleep after everyone left. The longer I sat there the more depressed I became, thinking about what he said and the way my life was going. There was nothing to look forward to anymore, only more emotional abuse and depression."

"I picked up the bottle of tranquilizers and took about twenty pills and called John at his office and when he answered I told him *Good-bye* and to tell the kids I love them. He hung up on me. That is the last thing I remembered until I woke up in the hospital and they were pumping out my stomach and working on me." More tears arrived.

A wave of empathy swept over me - her husband wanted her to kill herself and had manipulated her into a total state of despair. What a creep! Engineer John's greatest fear was he would have to divide their considerable community estate with his wife and pay her child support for many years. Even though he had a cold relationship with his children, he did not want to have to pay child support to an ex-wife.

I agreed to represent her on what I knew would be a bitter jury trial for custody. Her husband's lawyer specialized in child custody cases and I knew he was going to spoon feed the suicide attempt to the jury in an effort to show Joann was too emotionally unstable to raise their two children.

Early the next morning I arrived to find Jimmy again sitting in his pickup truck outside my office front door. I groaned under my breath. He was wide-awake this time and when he saw me drive up he waved a small envelope at me and jumped out of his truck and met me at the office door.

"Got those photos!" He seemed quite proud of himself. "You aren't going to believe your eyes." He was correct.

Over a cup of badly needed coffee I looked at the four Polaroid photos in amazement.

The first photo showed the hairy tops of *three* heads under the bed sheet. The second photo showed the sheet tossed back and three wide-eyed faces expressing shock and fright starring into the camera - two young men on either side of a young woman. The third photo showed two naked teenage boys bounding out of the opposite sides of the bed and even more features of a totally nude woman. The fourth photo showed only the young woman sitting up fully in bed with her hands over her face and the nude backsides of the two fleeing boys.

I was a little at a loss as to what to say so I asked in a quiet professional voice: "Do you recognize the three people?"

His response was immediate and heated, "My wife and the two teenage boys who live next door. They are sixteen and seventeen year old brothers."

"Well, I guess your mystery is solved, so what do you want me to do about all this?" as I asked and put him on the spot.

"I want a divorce and I want custody of my three girls as fast as possible, and I don't care about what it will cost."

I explained the need to move fast since a race to the courthouse would probably result now due to the wife's discovered orgy. The first parent to file a divorce would probably be given temporary custody of three girls until a full jury trial would result in a permanent custody order concerning the children.

We discussed legal fees and expenses and what provisions Jimmy would make for care of his girls when he was working. Luckily his mother lived nearby and he was going to move in with her immediately. She was available to care for the three young girls while Jimmy was working, assuming he had temporary custody. It was also important that a mature woman was available to care for the needs of three young girls.

I called in a secretary and dictated an affidavit for Jimmy to sign which basically stated the health and morals of the three young girls had been endangered by their mother's recent activities of allowing underage males to engage in illicit sex in the family home. Of course, the mother had also engaged in statutory rape with the teenage boys, which were felony offenses and another matter for her to worry about.

A divorce petition with attachments was soon typed and hand carried by me to the nearest district court judge in order to have that all powerful temporary restraining and child custody orders signed – which entitled Jimmy to immediate custody of his three daughters. Within three hours Jimmy was on his way to pick up his daughters along with a deputy sheriff to keep the peace while the deputy served the court papers on Jimmy's wife, Lisa. That custody case was soon set for jury trial since both parties wanted a quick trial.

Joann's custody case was also soon set on another district court's docket for jury trial. Joann's case was my main concern. I had to do some creative thinking about how to sway a jury into awarding the principal custody of two children to a mother who had tried unsuccessfully to do away with herself. I knew the husband had a cold calculating type of personality, but how do you prove that to a twelve-person jury and convince them that the mother is the most suitable person to have principle custody of the two children when she had supposedly tried to kill herself?

There was no evidence that either the father or mother had been deficient as parents. The entire case boiled down to the so-called suicide attempt and the husband's efforts to take advantage of that situation to gain custody.

Pre-trial discovery by the husband's attorney had focused on Joann's medications and her suicidal tendencies. I needed to address that matter directly with the jury and make sure that by the end of the trial, the jury had grown tired of hearing of the matter and were more focused on what kind of man drives a woman and mother to the point of such an act.

I decided to focus the entire trial on the fact that she was really screaming for help from her husband and his only reaction was to encourage her to kill herself. I knew that if I could prove to that jury the husband was trying to convince her wife that suicide was her best course of conduct that the jury would be repulsed by his actions and award the children to the more human and caring parent, the mother.

I started building a time line of the events on the day of the so-called suicide attempt. I subpoenaed the phone records of the parties and John's business phone and all the police and ambulance records of the event. I subpoenaed as witnesses, the EMT personnel to the trial to testify to what they discovered at the scene and the behavior of the husband.

After a jury was sworn and empanelled, the testimony began. The husband had filed the case so he was the moving party and had to put his evidence on before the wife. His evidence was exhaustive in its quantity and the quality, mostly addressing his child raising plans. The husband planned to enroll his children in a private school and hire a nanny to provide care and comfort at home during the times he was away from home.

The husband testified at length about plans to take the children to various amusement parks during the summer vacations. His testimony revealed the cold precision of an engineer's planning. I watched his demeanor closely and saw him exhibit the traits his wife had described in great detail – a cold, calculating asshole with no feelings for anyone but himself. I saw no sympathy for him developing in the jury's eyes. Everything he placed in evidence was too neatly arranged and contrived; it was as if he was composing a marketing plan for a product he was going to create.

On cross-examination I set the stage by asking him bluntly – "Did you tell your wife to kill herself on the morning in question?" He smiled and calmly replied, "Of course not - I would never do such a thing." I rose and walked over to stand next to the jury box – which caused the witness to have to face those twelve sets of eyes. "What time did you leave for work that morning?"

"About seven in the morning, the usual time - arrived at work at fifteen minutes to eight."

"Did you get a call from your wife that morning shortly after you got to work?" I asked.

He looked down at the floor – "I may have, I am not sure."

"Do you remember your wife telling you she had just taken a bottle of tranquilizers at your suggestion?"

"No, I do not," his voice cracking and angry.

"Did you talk to your wife again that day?" I asked.

"No, I called home before leaving work that day, about three o'clock, but got no answer."

"Did that alarm you when she did not answer the phone?" I asked.

"No. I thought she was probably outside the house."

"When did you arrive home?"

"About four o'clock."

"Did you locate your wife at home?"

"Yes. I could not open the doors to the house; she had dead-bolted the doors from inside. I saw her lying on our bed through the bedroom window and called the fire department and ambulance from a neighbor's house.

"How long did it take them to get to your house, you live out in the country, right?"

"About thirty minutes," he answered quietly – still staring at the floor, avoiding me.

"If you could not get in your house how did you think the fire department was going to get in?"

"I wasn't sure and did not know what else to do," he said.

"Did you suspect she had killed herself?" I asked.

"I did not know what happened to her," he replied.

"Why didn't you break a window or break down a door to gain entrance?" I asked and looked at the jurors' faces and saw some nodding heads, which was what I wanted to see.

"I did not know what to do Mr. Wilson – she could have simply been asleep for all I know."

"Did you run to any of your neighbors' houses seeking help," I asked.

"No, I just asked to use their phone," was his reply.

"How did the Fire Department gain access to your house?"

"They pried the back door off its hinges and went in with the paramedics and loaded up my wife and took her to the hospital."

"Mr. Scott, isn't it a fact that you wanted your wife to kill herself? Didn't you encourage her to do so? Isn't it true that she called you at eight o'clock that morning to tell you she had taken a bottle of tranquilizers; told you goodbye and take care of her babies?" I was in his face.

"No, never happened," was his cold reply.

I handed him the subpoenaed phone records from his house – and pointed out the call made to his work phone from his home phone at eight o'clock – a one-minute call.

"What did your wife say to you that morning?"

"I don't remember if she said anything to me that morning," he replied.

I see no other calls to or from that home phone that day, isn't that correct?" I asked.

"That's what the records show – I thought I called her about three o'clock."

"There is no indication on your phone records of such a call – it would be listed on the phone records at your home if she didn't answer, would it not?" I asked.

"I would not know," he replied.

"You expected her to be dead when you arrived home, didn't you?" I asked loudly, "Guess you were disappointed, weren't you?"

The look he gave me was that of a cornered rat – he was unable to come up with an answer – he just glared at me. Finally his lawyer came to his rescue – objecting to my "badgering the witness." Court overruled. I passed the witness and his lawyer rested their case.

I called the first responder to reach the scene – a volunteer fireman who lived in the neighborhood who heard the call over his scanner radio.

"Where did you find Mr. Scott when you arrived at his house?"

"He was sitting in his car. I ran up with a fire axe in my hands and asked where the victim was. Mr. Scott pointed to his house – said all the doors were all dead-bolted and please don't ruin his front door – try the back door. I ran around and forced the back door open and ran to the master bedroom and checked her vitals and she had shallow breathing and a weak pulse. I tried to wake her and she was non-responsive. The paramedics arrived then and took her to the nearest hospital."

"Did you have any more contact with her husband?"

No sir, never saw him again."

I then called my client to the stand and she testified about her dysfunctional marriage and her great love for her two children. She testified to her medical training and years of experience as a registered nurse. She told her story of a failed marriage to the jury.

"Our loveless marriage had evolved over the last year or so and my husband exhibited a constant coldness toward me. His comments about my appearance and value as a human being, as a wife, and as a mother were always negative."

I asked her – "Based on your experience with medications as a registered nurse – did you ingest enough of your tranquilizers to kill yourself?"

"No, I took too many and should not have done it, but I wanted John to react and come to my rescue and show some feelings for me. I was very depressed and wanted his attention and love – but, he just wanted me dead!" The tears started and the judge adjourned court for the day. I watched the jurors file out and noted the wet eyes of several of the women jurors.

The trial continued for several more days with relatives on both sides testifying about the various merits and demerits of each parent. My last witness dropped a big bomb on the husband and he never even knew the effect of his testimony. They were big football buddies and lived next door to each other. I had questioned the neighbor about why his phone number appeared on the husband's work phone records the same day that Joann was found unconscious in her home.

The neighbor testified, "I called John at work when Joann wouldn't answer her door that day to see if she was all right. I was returning some tools I borrowed several days earlier and noticed Joann had not brought in her mail or picked up their newspaper. That alarmed me and I called him to see if his wife was home since her car was there."

Then came the bombshell: "John told me Joann was fine – he had just spoken to her on the phone."

There was an audible sigh from the courtroom and I turned to the judge and announced, "We rest our case, your honor."

Closing arguments soon followed. I knew the husband's lawyer was a great storyteller and would try to wrap the jury's mind around a father's love for his children in his closing argument. The lawyer was also rude and made it a habit to make some type of scene in the courtroom when the other party's lawyer was giving his closing arguments.

Sure enough, I had just begun my closing argument to the jury when John's lawyer loudly pushed back his chair and walked out of the courtroom – leaving a young associate with his client. The jury's eyes followed the lawyer out of the courtroom and then shifted to me to watch my reaction.

I was ready – "The lawyer representing the husband is a fine storyteller and he will soon stand on a certain spot near you folks." I walked over to the right corner of the jury box and stopped. "This is the spot. He will then turn to you jurors and tell you a tear-jerking story about a father's love for his children, and the tears will flow down his face – it is all an act – I have seen it many times before, so just keep your minds focused on the evidence and not on the hot air of some smooth talking lawyer."

I summed up the evidence that supported my theory that my client was the victim of emotional abuse and a vengeful husband who wanted a divorce, but did not want to have to pay child support to his wife, so he had tried to destroy her as a human being and drive her to do away with herself.

"She knew she wasn't taking enough pills to kill herself and she was just screaming for help in her own way – a way she now knows is improper and will not happen again. She is a good person, a fine mother, and certainly fit to care for her two children as she has since their birth. You have heard not one word to the contrary."

The other lawyer returned to his seat as I finished my argument, and he immediately jumped up and loudly walked to exactly the spot I had forecasted, planted his feet and began his argument. "I want to tell you jurors a little story about a father's love for his children."

All twelve sets of eyes shifted from his face to look at me. I smiled and gave a little nod and the jurors smiled and several of them put their hands to their mouths to stifle their amusement. The lawyer stopped his argument, turned and looked at me, then looked up at the smiling judge.

"Did I say something funny, your honor?" he asked.

"No sir, let's move on counsel, please," the judge said and looked down at his notes.

The jury returned with a verdict in two hours, awarding custody of the children to Joann. She tearfully hugged me and each juror after court was adjourned. In a child custody trial – the jury's verdict on which parent is awarded custody of minor children is binding on everyone, even on the presiding judge. Joann continued on with her life as a single parent and good mother.

I barely had time to catch my breath, several days later a court clerk called Jimmy's custody case to trial in the Fort Worth domestic relations court. All parties and counsel were ordered to appear the next morning at nine to select a jury to hear that case. I packed up my briefcase with legal briefs, called my client, and alerted our witnesses to be ready to appear in court in the next day or so.

The lawyer for Jimmy's wife had filed numerous motions to suppress the four photos we had of the young mother and her young lovers. Her lawyer was afraid of possible criminal charges being filed if she took the stand and had to testify about her little romp in the hay. He wanted the photos suppressed.

The judge overruled the wife's motions and looked at her lawyer sternly. "This custody matter needs to be settled before I have to refer the evidence introduced at trial to the district attorney's office for review."

The lawyers and both their clients immediately withdrew to the nearby conference room and almost everyone was shocked when the wife suddenly said – "I don't want the fucking kids – I am going to join the Navy next week and all of you can go to hell!"

She walked over to her lawyer, whispered something in his ear and walked out of the room.

Her lawyer looked at me and Jimmy and shrugged his shoulders. "The only thing she asks for is that she not to have to pay any child support. She will give up the house and car – she will only take her clothes and personal items."

My client agreed to everything and it was dictated to the court reporter. It was approved by the judge who said, "He would let dead dogs lie," and not refer the matter to the D.A. My client was delighted and left in a rush to go tell the good news to his mother and his daughters.

I just wanted to go have a drink and forget the entire mess. I would like to say that everyone lived happily ever after – but they didn't. The story does not end there – but it should have. Lisa did join the Navy and sailed away. Jimmy and his girls did not hear from Lisa for one year - no cards or phone calls.

One day Jimmy called me with bad news, "She is back – the Navy kicked her out and she is pregnant and she wants to know if I will let her have the three girls over the Christmas holidays," – Jimmy's voice showed his unease about that arrangement.

Lisa had no court-ordered visitation with her three daughters – everything had been left open-ended in the divorce decree *"visitation was to be at the agreement of the parties"* because no one knew then what her Navy schedule was going to be.

I felt a chill go down my back. This woman was a loose cannon and I expressed my first thoughts strongly to him, "She is probably going to grab the girls and head for the border – you will probably never see your daughters again. Jimmy, do not let her take those girls out of your sight. Either you or your mother always need to be with the children when Lisa is around."

Jimmy agreed and the conversation ended, but not the trouble.

A month later I was driving on a nearby country road, one of those country roads that is full of frequent turns and shape curves. Suddenly, a car traveling at too high a rate of speed roared around me in a no passing zone. I commented to my passenger, "That is one dangerous driver, looks like a woman and a car full of children. She better slow down or someone is going to be killed."

A few minutes later, I rounded a sharp curve and was greeted by the sickening sight of an overturned vehicle in the middle of the road. The vehicle was smoking and two wheels still spinning. Bodies were hanging out of the vehicle and lying in the roadway, several of which were covered in blood.

I jumped out of my car, directed my passenger to drive to a nearby fire station to summon help. I ran to try to give aid to the injured.

The driver, a woman who looked familiar to me, was now trying to pull herself out the car window and she appeared not to be seriously injured but she smelled strongly of booze and was mumbling something to herself. She had many cuts and scrapes and her clothes were torn and bloody.

No one in the car had worn seat belts. It looked like there were three large rag dolls scattered around the overturned car. Closer examination revealed the dolls were young girls, all unconscious and with head and probable internal injuries. I did not move any of them and only tried to stop the bleeding that was coming from numerous deep gashes in their torn bodies.

I was soon holding a small hand in each of my trembling hands trying to talk to them as I choked back tears – a more gut-wrenching scene you cannot imagine. One small girl's chest seemed to be completely crushed and she was struggling for breath and obviously in very critical condition. The injured woman seemed uninterested and dazed and she stumbled around the scene, mumbling.

The EMT's arrived in minutes and took over and a parade of ambulances and police cars soon appeared. I was so shaken by the experience that I left the area as soon as possible.

I contacted the police department the next day and gave them what information I could provide. It was then I learned the identity of the woman and the three young girls. It was Jimmy's ex-wife, Lisa, and he had let her have the three girls to see Lisa's mother for Christmas. One girl had died. The other two survived, but with serious injuries.

The ex-wife had no serious injuries and only a driving while intoxicated charge to contend with.

I never heard from Jimmy again. I think he was too embarrassed and ashamed to speak to me again. I will never forget that horrific scene of those three broken dolls lying in that roadway.

Joann called me one day - several months later and invited me over to her house for dinner, I politely declined. I never heard from her again, either.

Sometimes marriages do not last, but children born to those marriages do last a lifetime. Parents who become divorced should never say bad things about each other to their children. Each child wants a mother and a father – and only they will decide whom they love and respect.

I don't think you can make a lawyer honest by an act of legislature. You've got to work on his conscience. And his lack of conscience is what makes him a lawyer.
Will Rogers.

13

I BEGAN TO NOTICE THAT THE MORE jury trials I participated in, the more potential clients walked in my office door. The best word of mouth publicity a young lawyer can obtain is that of an impressed jury member – he tells his family, his neighbors and everyone who will listen – about the gutsy young barrister who went the extra mile for his client and won the day.

One summer I tried twelve jury cases in twelve weeks – only losing one verdict. A new trial started every Monday in a different court of several surrounding county courthouses.

Most lawyers try to disappear during the summer months – advising the courts in advance what months they will be on vacation – with their families, of course. I was hell-bent to get justice for my clients even at the great cost to my own family life – my wife and growing children saw little of me. An ambitious lawyer can often cause grief to his family by his absence.

I had just completed a jury trial when one of the women jurors appeared in my office.

"Can you please help my older sister, Joan, she was brain damaged in a serious car wreck and no lawyer will take her case."

I heard that tale many times – most lawyers avoid difficult negligence cases – too much work for an unknown outcome.

"What are the facts of her case?" I asked.

"She was driving home from work in Fort Worth at four thirty in the afternoon when a large truck pushed her small compact car into the median railing on I-35 expressway. Her vehicle went airborne and rolled and she suffered severe brain injuries. She never saw the truck that knocked her vehicle into the median."

"How does she know a truck hit her?" I asked – already seeing the problems in this case.

"Another driver saw what happened and rendered aid to my sister. He only saw a large flatbed truck, with a red cab, with a load of lumber. The truck never even slowed down and was soon out of sight in the heavy traffic."

"So, if I understand what you are saying – your sister has serious brain injuries – never saw who hit her vehicle – and the only witness says the wreck was caused by a large flat-bed truck hauling lumber – which had a red cab – is that correct?"

"That's it in a nutshell – we have talked to a dozen lawyers – they all declined to help," she said, watching me for any signs of interest.

"This is the problem from a legal standpoint – in order to recover damages in this type of wreck – we call it a negligence case – the burden of proof is on your sister and her lawyer to prove by a majority of the evidence that the operator of that lumber truck failed to exercise ordinary care in the operation of his truck that day. And, that his failure to exercise care was the cause of your sister's car wreck and her injuries."

"From what you have told me – it would appear the truck driver failed to keep a proper lookout and failed to stay in his lane of traffic – and that is the cause of your sister losing control of her vehicle and being forced into the concrete median of the freeway. The big problem is – how do you prove who was the owner-operator of that red truck without any evidence?"

She looked disappointed at my comments and raised her voice, "But my sister's life is ruined, she will be an invalid forever and she did nothing wrong – and the guilty driver got away Scott-free – it ain't right! Isn't there anything you can do to help her?"

"Leave the police report and let me think about it awhile – I will be in touch. I noticed the two year statute of limitations is expiring in a few months," I said.

She was happy I did not reject the case outright and was going to put some thought into it. She had a smile on her face when she left – it was my problem now and she felt a burden lifted.

I called Abe, my investigator into my office and explained the facts of this mystery. Abe was a retired navy man with the tattoos and beer-drinking ability to prove it. He also had the bloodhound and bulldog determination a good investigator must possess.

We looked at the facts we knew and what we needed to know. We had a red-cabbed lumber truck – probably making a delivery in the Fort Worth area. We hoped it was not an out of town truck.

"Abe, make a list of all the lumberyards in the Fort Worth area and visit each of them and see which ones have red-cabbed delivery trucks."

The next day Abe reported back; all the lumberyards had at least one or more red-cabbed delivery trucks.

"O.K., Abe – this wreck occurred on a Friday afternoon at four thirty let's see if possibly this truck was really heading back to its lumber yard for the night – so set up a surveillance on that stretch of freeway this Friday between four and five o'clock and follow any large lumber delivery truck with a red cab you might encounter.

That Friday afternoon – Able hit pay dirt – he called in an excited voice – "I found the lumber company." He related that shortly before five o'clock a red-cabbed lumber delivery truck drove past the scene of the prior wreck at a very high rate of speed – well over the posted speed limit and was weaving in and out of traffic. Abe followed the truck to a local lumber company and noted that all that company's delivery trucks had red cabs.

The next day I made a pretext call to that lumber company and told them I had lost all my records for a lumber delivery – by chance on the same day and time of the wreck in question. The lady looked in her records and confirmed one of their delivery trucks made deliveries in that part of town that afternoon but that I must be mistaken on the date – since she couldn't locate my delivery.

I called my new clients and accepted the case.

A suit was immediately filed against that particular lumber company and I subpoenaed the trucking company delivery records for the day in question. I was able to determine which delivery truck was the probable culprit.

The driver of that truck was soon subpoenaed to a deposition and admitted that – *he may have forced another vehicle into the guardrail on the occasion in question. He had not stopped because his vision was blocked by other traffic and he was unsure what had occurred behind him.*

That admission was enough to raise a fact question for a jury's determination concerning what had caused the woman's injuries. That fact coupled with the proof that the truck was at the wreck location at the time of the wreck created that majority of evidence needed to establish liability in the case.

The successful conclusion to this case closely following Sonny's settlement brought to Abe's mind that old Navy Seabee saying, "The difficult we do immediately – the impossible takes a little longer."

I often shake my head in disgust when I see some lawyers – really ambulance chasers – with ads on the radio or T.V. saying, "Hire us if you are hurt in an accident." Such ads cheapen the legal profession to the level of used car sales pitches. A good lawyer does not need to advertise his services – his skills in a courtroom will produce all the clients he will ever need. Besides, there are no recoveries for *accident* victims – there are only recoveries for victims of someone's *negligence*. An accident is not negligence – just the opposite: negligence is preventable, while an accident is not.

*There is no better way to exercise the imagination than
the study of the law. No artist ever interpreted
nature as freely as a lawyer interprets the truth.*
Jean Giradoux

14

BY THE MID-EIGHTIES I HAD TRIED ENOUGH criminal cases in the Dallas County Criminal Courts to know I didn't want to play their games anymore. There is something wrong with a district attorney's office that brags it can *convict a ham sandwich* for any crime committed in Dallas County. Talk about a hostile work environment for defense lawyers.

If a defense lawyer announced that he would not accept the state's preset plea bargain for his client - he was immediately informed by the judge – usually a former prosecutor himself, and the prosecutor assigned to that case – that "Your client is going to receive the max if you do not get with the program."

The Dallas County juries usually were rubber stamps for the prosecutors. Many innocents went to jail or prison - the end product of prosecutor over-kill, timid defense lawyers and the judges' apathy or active participation in the injustices.

One case of mine comes to mind. A thirty-five year old walking cripple retained my services to defend him on a driving under the influence charge. He had a clean record but the two prosecutors assigned to his case wanted blood – and another notch in their gun belts.

The facts were uncontested. My client had just been released from the Dallas Veteran's hospital and drove directly into a police roadblock. Darryl had slurred his words to the patrolman and was arrested when he admitted he was taking strong pain pills and was a little dizzy.

Darryl had been shot nine times while serving in the Vietnam War. His body was road kill. He could not walk well or speak clearly. His body was held together only by metal plates and pins. He spent his days fishing at the local lakes and had no family.

His doctor had placed him on heavy pain medication on the day in question, after some follow-up surgery. Darryl should have had a driver that day.

I related my client's tale of woe to the two prosecutors and they simply handed me the standard plea of guilty paperwork for such an offense. Thirty days in jail and suspension of driving privileges for one year.

I declined and was promptly informed my client would soon become *toast* and a guest of the county jail for six months at the least and two years of suspended driving privileges for his first offense.

A grueling jury trial followed, and while the jury was in deliberations, I was killing time walking the so-called halls of justice when I stumbled into a young blonde woman buying a soft drink at the snack bar. She looked at me and I at her – we knew each other but could not place where we had met. After a few minutes talking it dawned on me. When she was fifteen and I was twenty-five, she would flirt with me while her mother shopped in a local Safeway Store where I then worked - it is a small world.

We talked about old times and she was surprised to learn I was a lawyer now. I was equally shocked to know that the former high school freshman was now a judge's administrative assistant. I had thought she would probably end up working as a waitress somewhere or as a homemaker with five children. She was married but *had refused to have children* – which was causing problems with her hapless husband. She demanded we have a drink across the street as soon as her office closed in a short time.

The jury soon returned with a guilty verdict in my client's case – but, they took mercy on Darryl and probated the minimum sentence and he left the courthouse a happy free man with his driving privileges intact.

I walked across the street to a local pub and met with Sherry for a drink. I soon learned she could put away a lot of booze quickly and she was fairly drunk in less than an hour. She then really loosened her tongue and brought me up to date about the gossip making the rounds in the local criminal courts.

"Some of the judges are sleeping with their prosecutors," she blurted out.

It took my mind a few moments to digest that comment and realize its full implications.

Women were starting to take an interest in the practice of law and a few women lawyers were then becoming prosecutors – but the change had been so gradual I had never really thought much about the new dynamic that was entering the world of criminal justice – sex!

Sex between the lawyers, sex between the prosecutors, and most sinister – sex between judges and prosecutors assigned to the same criminal courtrooms.

I had graduated law school in 1973 in a class of one hundred fifteen men and five women. That male-female ratio had radically changed over the years to become roughly equal by the mid-eighties.

I looked into Sherry's glazed eyes and wondered if she had any realization of what she had just told me. I pressed her on the subject. "You have got to be kidding me, are you saying that some of the female prosecutors are having sex with their criminal court judges, in the same courts they are assigned?"

"Yes," she blurted. "In one court the judge and his prosecutor shack-up at that hotel across the street - during their lunch breaks or when their juries are out deliberating."

My head was spinning. "Are they married to other people?"

"Oh yes! Many times I have to make excuses for certain judges when their frantic wives are looking for them."

I was surprised that such behavior had not caused a public scandal by now – law licenses would have been revoked, criminal convictions over turned – marriages ruined.

"How do they keep a lid on it?" I asked.

"No one blows the whistle on anyone in this courthouse, so nothing ever happens-it's like a little Peyton Place." She shrugged.

I pressed her for names – trying to pin her down – she never hesitated and started naming judges and their female prosecutors by name.

Several names I knew and it suddenly made sense to me why those female prosecutors seemed to do and say anything they wished in those particular courts without fear of their judges' rebukes – which never came.

I made myself a promise that day – never to accept another criminal case that was going to result in a trial in a Dallas County criminal court – now that I knew the true grit. I would not allow one of my clients to receive an unfair trial due to such courtroom behavior as had just been related to me; I would have had to blow the whistle – which would have been the end of my law practice in Dallas County, at the very least.

My own daughter was now in college herself, working her way toward law school admission. She wanted to join the noble profession and follow in her father's footsteps. She had no clue of my own youthful history or what the practice of law was really all about. She had watched several of my criminal jury trials and once remarked in my ear at the end of one of my emotional closing arguments that had several women jurors in tears. "You would have made a good actor." She had no idea what a heavy burden a client's life or fortune is, but would find out for herself someday.

One of the Dallas County female prosecutors who was active in the criminal courts during this time period was a woman about my age named Catherine Crier. She would go on to become a Dallas County District Judge before she moved into the T.V. news media business and become a celebrity in her own right. I had no reason to doubt her virtue as a prosecutor, since she would never return my smiles when we happened to be on the elevators together. She appeared too upright to involve herself in such lascivious behavior as was occurring around her.

I was disappointed when she published her own book in 2002, *The Case Against Lawyers,* about the practice of law, and never mentioned what was really occurring in the Dallas County Criminal Courts. She must have been above it all - or was afraid of the firestorm she would create for her brother and sister prosecutors and judges if she blew the whistle on the ole' crew.

I stayed in casual contact with Sherry for the next year or so – mostly phone calls or an occasional cocktail. She would update me on the continuing soap operas of the judge-prosecutor sex escapades. It never ceased to amaze me that such behavior could go on in a city as big as Dallas and be kept "under wraps." In Fort Worth the criminal courts erupted in scandal during the same time period with reports of certain criminal judges trading sex favors from female defendants in exchange for dismissal of their criminal cases. Those matters became front-page news for months in the Fort Worth media - followed by criminal trials of some of those actors. But, then again, Fort Worth and Dallas are as different as night and day – in more ways than one.

There were rumors and muted conversations about innocents being framed and convicted in those Dallas criminal courts by overzealous prosecutors and lying cops in those days. The district attorney and his chief deputies were able to keep the lid tightly secure for many years. The juries always fell in line and did their law and order duties of following the dubious evidence to a final conviction. The Court of Criminal Appeals of Texas rubber stamped everything and thereby betrayed their oaths of office.

It would all rot away twenty years later when DNA evidence became admissible in the Dallas courts and the long process of releasing previously convicted Dallas prisoners who were innocent, began.

*My decision to become a lawyer was irrevocably sealed when I
realized my father hated the legal profession.*
John Grisham

15

ABE, MY ACE INVESTIGATOR, REQUESTED ME TO *please take a few minutes
to discuss with him two topics of great concern to him: his
health and his drinking buddy's marital problems.* So, one
morning at seven o'clock while the office was still quiet we
poured coffee and talked.

Abe had been complaining for several months of pain in
his groin area. He had gone to his family doctor and been
diagnosed as having a bad strain. Abe's wife, a registered
nurse, concurred, reminding Abe he had been carrying
too heavy of loads of lumber when he was busy adding an
additional bedroom to their home to house their newborn
baby boy - in addition to their older son, who was my own
son's age and his friend.

"Bob, my pain is getting worse, not better, and it is
causing me to drink more to try to ease the pain and the
pain pills just don't help."

I had been telling Abe to go see a urologist for weeks – I
knew his family doctor to be a worthless excuse for a doctor
because of the steady stream of his complaining patients
who came into my office.

I suspected that Abe's complaints were of a more serious
nature – since Abe was not the type of person to complain
of minor pain - he had single-handedly built their home and
suffered the many minor injuries that could be expected
from such an undertaking.

"Abe, you go right now and don't come back to work
until you see a specialist and that is an order," I said and

meant it. He concurred and promised to leave shortly to find medical evaluation as soon as he related his neighbor's dilemma to me.

"Roy is my poker playing buddy. Every Saturday for years we've gotten together with two other neighbors to play poker and drink beer. The problem is Roy's wife, Martha. She has thrown him out of their house and filed a divorce. She wants custody of their six children and wants Roy to pay child support. Roy is so depressed he can't even look for a job or play poker anymore. I am afraid he is going to do away with himself. Can you represent him? He doesn't want a divorce. He is heartbroken."

"Abe, you know I hate divorce cases. Get one of our other attorneys to represent Roy," I said, hoping that solved the problem.

"Roy doesn't have any money, Martha handled all the money – he has never worked!"

"Never worked – how old is this guy?" I asked.

"He is fifty-five years old – his wife is the bread winner and she controls the purse and everything else," Abe said.

"Abe, we can't pay our bills and represent people for free – is that what you are asking me to do?"

"Take his fees out of my paycheck, I will stand good for it," Abe said – really putting me in an awkward situation.

"Abe – you know I would never do that – tell the guy to make an appointment to see me – I will do what I can, maybe you and him can do some repair work to this office to make up for my services," I said, knowing I was defeated.

"Thanks Bob – you will like Roy – great guy."

Abe left the office after making sure Roy had a firm appointment. That was to be Abe's last day of work. The specialist he saw immediately sent him to the hospital for testing which confirmed their worst fears – widespread cancer. His doctors told him to get his affairs in order – he had six months to live. He called me and gave me the bad news and broke down over the phone. I was shocked that a strong and healthy looking man still in his early forties could be so fragile and vulnerable to such an illness. I thought of his two sons and devoted wife having to make it alone in life.

Abe was immediately placed on chemotherapy, a last ditch effort to save his life.

Roy appeared for his appointment and he was a living – breathing example of one helpless, depressed man with no future. Roy's story was certainly different than most.

"I never worked. I just stayed home with the kids. Mom did it all. She never asked me to do a thing, just stay out of her way. I wonder why she even married me. I think she felt sorry for me after my mom died. I was lost and she found me and married me almost thirty years ago."

"What does your wife – Martha – do for a living?" I asked – wondering to myself how I was going to impress a judge with my client's history.

"She operates a dairy farm – milks cows – sells the milk and all that. And, oh yes, she also throws newspapers each morning and each night – you know, paper routes." Roy stated very matter-of-factly.

I wasn't sure I heard Roy correctly – I knew from my youth the work involved running a dairy business – milking and feeding cows morning and evening – a fulltime job in itself – for several people.

"You mean she has two paper routes and also milks cows twice a day?" I asked.

"Yeah, she is a real workhorse. She never stops. Our oldest children now help out with the cattle milking, but she runs the show." I was now convinced I was on the wrong side of this lawsuit.

"So why did she throw you out after all these years?" I asked.

"She just came home one night from throwing papers and I was having a beer and a smoke and she looked at me kind of strange and said – *"It's over – get your lazy ass out of my house"* – and packed my suitcase and threw us both out of the front door."

"How do your children feel about all this?"

"They are as shocked as me. They miss me playing card games and watching TV with them. I had to move in with my grandpa to have a place to live. I have no income or job."

I shook my head and wondered how all of this would play out in court. I told Roy to look for a job – which I knew was a hopeless endeavor for a man who had never worked.

Abe's condition deteriorated quickly – due in large part to the poison being pumped into his veins. His two hundred fifty pound bulldog frame soon began to look like a frail old man. He asked me to do his Last Will and Testament, which I did. He constantly marked the days off the calendar and pointed out how many days remained of the one hundred and eighty days given him by God's men on earth – his doctors.

I always reminded him that "No one knows how long they have on this earth" – but he had it firmly planted in his mind that he was a dying man – and sure enough, he passed away exactly six months from the day of his diagnosis with his family and I watching and waiting. It was a great loss to all involved.

Roy's divorce was called to trial and the parties with all six children – from young to almost grown appeared in court for the final hearing. Martha had filed the divorce – so she took the stand first and related for several hours the marital history of her working fourteen hours a day, each day of their marriage – while Roy entertained the children at home.

Martha emphasized the point that she not only had to do all the work, earn all the income, pay all the bills – *she also had to do all the cookin' and cleanin'*. Roy essentially did *nothin' but sit on his behind* - as Martha related earnestly from the witness stand.

After Martha had convinced the judge and everyone listening that Roy was really a miserable excuse for a husband and provider – her lawyer passed Martha to me for any cross-examination.

The evidence introduced in court that day reminded me of the old Ma and Pa Kettle movies in which Pa Kettle relied completely on his loud-mouth, but hard working wife for shelter and provisions. This courtroom scene of this very large, and very loud woman, sitting with her arms folded to her chest while her hung-dog looking husband sat helpless next to me was right out of a Norman Rockwell painting.

I stood and walked behind my client and looked up at Martha whose mouth was busy chewing her loudly popping gum and glaring at me from the witness stand. I had to bite my lip to keep from smiling at her. All their children could be heard whispering excitedly to each other behind me in the benches as they waited in anticipation to see their Mom make a fool out of me. You would have thought they were watching a professional wrestling match and I was about to be thrown out of the ring.

"Martha – you run the ranch – wouldn't that be true?" I asked.

"What's that supposed to mean – I run the ranch? I do all the work and earn the living is that what you are talkin' about?" She leaned forward in her chair – ready for combat.

"You will agree your husband has no skills and is completely dependent on you for survival?

"That's correct – he is useless as tits on a boar hog," she replied.

A few snickers could be heard from behind me from the children.

I placed my two hands on the back of my slumping client's shoulders.

"Martha, you have been married to this man for over thirty years – he loves you dearly – his children love him and you now want to throw him into the street like a piece of garbage – how do you think that looks to the Man upstairs?" I asked – pointing my finger to the sky.

The courtroom suddenly became very quiet, even the gum popping stopped.

Martha's face suddenly lost all its color and she cast her eyes to her booted feet and her facial expression suddenly changed from anger to one of softness.

She started again with the furious gum chewing and the loud popping continued. She looked up at me – then looked at Roy's moist eyes and she struggled to speak.

"I never thought about it that way – he is pretty helpless, I guess it's my burden to take care of this man – God has ordained it," she said in a much softer tone.

I applied the pressure. "Martha – you two still love each other – what in the world is going to happen to Roy if you abandon him? What about your wedding vows - for the good times and the bad times?"

Martha again looked down at her worn boots as if they held the answer to her dilemma. The courtroom was quiet as a tomb. After several moments she looked up at the judge, tears starting to show on her sun burned cheeks.

"Judge – I dismiss my divorce – I will take him back – we can't live without each other – I made a choice and it is God's Will that we live out our lives together, he is my husband now and forever and my burden."

The Judge looked over at me – his eyes wide and amazed by Martha's statement.

"We join in her motion to dismiss, your honor – my client never wanted a divorce to start with - can everyone be excused?" I asked quickly, before Martha could change her mind.

"Case will be dismissed by consent of the parties," the grateful judge proclaimed and rose from the bench – "Good luck, ma'am," he said to Martha as she departed the witness stand to gather her happy band of loud children and administer a bear hug to poor Roy, who was weakly trying to pull himself together after his near death experience.

I drove back to my office that day with a smile on my face – Abe would have been proud of the results of his friend's court hearing. Abe had probably saved Roy's life by talking me into representing him that morning. Things happen for a reason.

After watching Abe slowly waste away while undergoing chemotherapy I became convinced the medical team deprived him of his last few months on earth with his family. Maybe he would have died anyway as his doctors predicted in six months, but if that was all the time he had left to live, why not let him enjoy those months instead of being very sick and miserable, not from cancer – but from the poison they pumped into his body. After all, who appointed them God Almighty? No one has the right or power to tell someone they have six months to live – not even the government.

God wanted to chastise mankind, so he sent lawyers.
Russian Proverb

16

By the mid-eighties I was becoming bored and burned out with the practice of law. There had to be more to life than daily fighting with lawyers, judges, and the system. I started searching for a less stressful way to make a living. Everyone had always told me that there is only so much land in the world and therefore a person can never go wrong by buying and owning as much real estate as you can beg, borrow or steal.

A year earlier I had bought a five-acre tract from a client who was desperate to sell at a bargain basement price. The property had a nice rental house on one end and good cattle pasture on the remaining acreage.

Six months later, the renter of the house died suddenly and his widow contacted me and wanted to buy the house for her and her two young children. She had cash from her husband's life insurance proceeds. She only wanted the house – not the acreage, could I help her out?

I agreed to partition the property and quoted her the same sales price for the house that the entire tract cost me. She heartily agreed and I soon owned four acres debt free and she was a happy homeowner.

A few weeks later a cattlewoman said she wanted to buy my four acres to raise some calves. I quoted her the same price I paid for the property and she agreed. I doubled my money – and had never even set foot on the property. It was all too easy.

It appeared to me that even a fool could make money in real estate. I had a very large line of unsecured credit at a bank where I served as bank counsel and a director. I would use it to make some easy money.

I needed a business partner who had a good head for business and like myself, wanted a new lease on life, less stress and more money. Ken was the manager of a large manufacturing plant in my area and we were good friends. I represented his company in a lawsuit against the local taxing authority.

Ken was also burned out with his management position and he jumped at my proposal to form a partnership to develop real estate. We started spending every possible moment looking for suitable tracts of land to develop. We soon found the perfect undeveloped tract of farmland, complete with old chicken coops, stinky hog pens, and thirty acres of tall weeds.

Using my line of bank credit we immediately purchased the property and retained a civil engineering firm to start the process of officially subdividing the entire tract and installing approved streets and utilities. Ken and I spent every weekend on rented tractors clearing the property of weeds, sheds, and old manure. It was hot, sweaty, and dirty work – and we loved every minute of it. Again our families suffered from absent husbands and fathers – but we were on a mission to free ourselves of our burden of professional slavery.

It took almost six months to have all the civil engineering and surveying work completed and another six months for official approval from various governmental agencies. By the end of the process we had used up most of our money-borrowing authority. We were now ready to begin building homes and join the ranks of the wealthy leisure classes.

We made arrangements with several financial lenders to start short-term financing of the new homes we were going to build and sell. Interest rates were sky high then – eighteen percent and higher. Soon construction crews and utility trucks were abundant and dirt was flying and concrete flowing and house frames being erected.

Several homes were completed to serve as our house models. We planned our grand opening – complete with free barbeque and black diamond watermelons – all catered at great cost.

Newspaper ads and radio announcements were purchased. Ken and I waited in great anticipation for the official opening of our development – planned for a Saturday and Sunday.

We enlisted our office staff and families to assist with the huge crowd of hungry homebuyers that we expected. At nine o'clock that Saturday morning we removed the barricades from the entry streets to our development and waited with great anticipation for the waves of expected cars and people.

No one appeared, not even a phone call. Our workers helped themselves to barbeque and watermelons while Ken and I checked to see why no one came to the grand opening. All the ads appeared in the local papers as planned – the radio spots had occurred. Still nothing happened on Saturday or Sunday. We gave away a lot of brisket and watermelons to anyone and everyone.

A great chill settled over Ken and I as we realized that our timing had been perfect – perfectly bad. We had managed to develop and open a major real estate project just as the Texas real estate market tanked thanks in no small part to the Federal Tax Reform Act of 1986 which single handedly destroyed the real estate, oil and gas, and horse business in Texas and many other states overnight. I learned the hard way that fortunes can be lost as quickly in real estate development as they can be made. Timing and location are everything.

Ken's wife threatened to divorce and leave him unless he walked away from our partnership, which he did, leaving me alone to deal with all the lenders and creditors demanding their money. Over the next several years I managed to liquidate the real estate and pay all the creditors in full at great cost to my own financial health.

The nation-wide Savings and Loan fiasco followed the real estate crash and as usual the federal government created more federal bureaucrats and agencies to administer the mess it had created.

I had no choice now but refocus on my law practice and do what I did best – litigate – until something better came along. I had violated that old adage – "Stay with what you know," and paid a high price.

In fifteen years my office had grown from one part-time receptionist to an office of six lawyers and a staff of thirteen. That is a lot of mouths to feed every two weeks. It required me to hit the ground running every morning. If I could have foreseen what awaited me in the next couple of years, I would have run further and faster.

...To be continued at: www.bobbystrials.com

Made in the USA
Middletown, DE
19 July 2018